Rarotonga

& the Cook Islands

a travel survival kit

Cook Islands – a travel survival kit

Published by
 Lonely Planet Publications
 PO Box 88, South Yarra, Victoria 3141, Australia
 Lonely Planet Publications
 PO Box 2001A, Berkeley, California, USA 94702

Printed by
 Colorcraft, Hong Kong

Photography
 Tony Wheeler (TW), Donald Cole/Cook Islands Tourist Authority (DC/CITA), and Cook Islands
  Tourist Authority (CITA) as indicated.
 Portraits/Flower page: Tony Wheeler and Cook Islands Tourist Authority
 Front cover: Tony Wheeler
 Back cover: Cook Islands Tourist Authority

Illustrations
 Historical: William Wyatt Gill, from *Cannibals and Converts*, *From Darkness to Light in Polynesia* and
  Cook Islands Custom, all published by the Institute of Pacific Studies, University of the South Pacific.
 Title page and Page 65: Rick Welland

National Library of Australia Cataloguing in Publication Data

Wheeler Tony, 1946-.
 Rarotonga & the Cook Islands, a travel survival kit

 First ed.
 Includes index
 ISBN 0 908086 97 0

 1. Cook Islands – Description and Travel – 1986 – Guide-books I. Title

919.6'2304

 © Tony Wheeler, 1986

Tony Wheeler

Born in England, Tony spent his school years in Pakistan, the West Indies and the USA, returning to England to do a university degree in engineering. After a short spell as an automotive design engineer he returned to university to do an MBA, then dropped out on the Asia overland trail with his wife Maureen. They set up Lonely Planet in the mid-70s and have been travelling, writing and publishing guidebooks ever since. On this visit to the Cook Islands their daughter Tashi (aged five) and son Kieran (aged three) helped with the research.

This Edition

Thanks to the Cook Islands Tourist Authority for the use of their colour transparencies and to Rick Welland for the title-page painting. On the island of Atiu, Roger Malcolm was enormously helpful and I had a wonderful time there. Thanks also to Atiu cave guides Tangi Jimmy and Tipuni Aukino. On Mangaia thanks must go to Kaokao Raeora and to cave guide George Tuara.

Back in Australia the Lonely Planet staff pitched in to produce this book: Richard Everist edited, Todd Pierce drew maps, designed and did the paste-up, Ann Logan typeset, and Hugh Finlay helped with proof reading and indexing.

And the Next

Things change, prices go up, good places go bad and bad ones go bankrupt. So if you find things better, worse or simply different please write and tell us about it. As usual good letters will be rewarded with a free copy of the next edition or an alternative Lonely Planet guidebook.

For the Technically Minded

For several years now all our Lonely Planet guidebooks have passed through a word-processor at some stage in their production. Many of them are written on word-processors, either on the Kaypro 2s, 4s, or 10s we use in-house or by any other type of word-processor that outside authors might have (some of them have Kaypros too). Editing of the author's completed text also takes place on Kaypros (we translate 'foreign' floppy disks into our Kaypro format). Finally the Kaypro disks are transmitted to our Itek Digitek typesetting equipment, the 'galleys' are produced and become the final book artwork. This book took electronic production a stage further. I took a Toshiba T1100 lap-top computer with me to the Cook Islands and wrote most of the book while I was there. I came back with the whole book on a single 3½ inch floppy disk, in my shirt pocket!

Contents

Introduction

The tiny and remote Cook Islands are Polynesia in a conveniently handy, though widely scattered, package. They offer something for nearly everyone. Rarotonga, the main island, has modern resort facilities, fine beaches, excellent restaurants, spectacular coral reefs, a wide variety of accommodation possibilities and good entertainment; all on an island just 32 km around. Furthermore it's a spectacularly beautiful island, a mountainous high island like Tahiti, cloaked in dense jungle. 'Raro' is also the entry point for 99% of visitors to the Cooks as it is the location for the international airport.

Rarotonga is only the starting point for exploring the Cook Islands. From 'Raro' you can fly or, if you're feeling hardy and adventurous and have time to spare, ship to the other islands of the southern group. Spectacularly beautiful Aitutaki is by far the best known with its huge lagoon fringed with tiny, picture-postcard islets. Aitutaki is a combination of high island and atoll and is a frequent nominee for

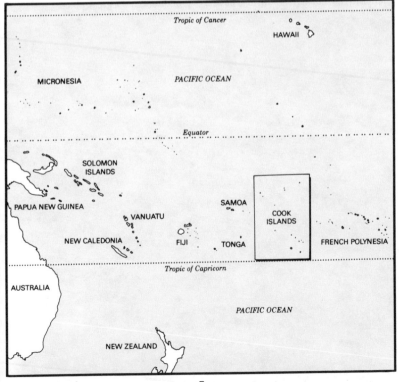

any 'most beautiful island in the Pacific' award. If Raro is the Tahiti of the Cooks then Aitutaki is the Bora Bora.

Few visitors go further than these two principal islands but that's a great shame because some of the others are equally interesting. Atiu and Mangaia are geological curiosities with a fringing raised fossil reef known as a *makatea*. On both islands the *makatea* is a weirdly beautiful area of razor-sharp coral formations absolutely riddled with limestone caves. Stalactites and stalagmites may seem a strange thing to find on a tropical island but the caves are full of them. There's also a cave on Atiu inhabited by a tiny, unique swallow known as the *kopeka* and which has countless burial caves. Mauke and Mitiaro, smaller islands in the southern group, also have a fringing *makatea* and can be visited from Rarotonga.

Finally there are the remote islands of the northern group, accessible only by the infrequent inter-island trading ships. These are the classic low atolls of the Pacific and you need time and persistence to explore them.

Of course islands aren't all there is to the Cooks, there are also the Cook Islanders themselves. Some say these handsome, easy-going people are the friendliest folk in the Pacific. They certainly have some of the most spectacular dancers and an evening at an Aitutaki 'island night' or a raucous Friday night at the Banana Court Bar in Rarotonga is an experience to remember. 'The Cooks are like Tahiti as it was 20 years ago,' say the promoters. It's a great place.

Facts about the Country

HISTORY

Although the Cook Islands only have a clearly recorded history from the time of the arrival of Europeans, archaeologists have discovered many early *marae* and traces of early settlements from a time when the population of Rarotonga was far greater than it is today. The ancient road known as the *Ara Metua* still encircles most of Rarotonga today and may be as much as a thousand years old. Rarotongans insist that their island was the jumping-off point from which the great Maori voyages were made to New Zealand. Indeed Rarotonga may be the Hawaikii of Polynesian migration legends. Modern historians believe that the Polynesian migrations moved through the islands in the 5th century AD, much earlier than the legends which date the first arrivals on the island around 1200 AD.

Polynesian Settlement

The Cook Islanders are Polynesians, people of the 'many' (*poly*) islands of the South Pacific. They are Maoris like the original settlers of New Zealand, and their language is also Maori, closely related to the language of the original New Zealanders and also to the Polynesian language of Tahiti or Hawaii.

It is thought that 40,000 years ago the Pacific region was totally uninhabited. Around that time people started to move down from Asia and settled Australia and Melanesia – the 'black islands' which include modern Papua New Guinea. The Australian Aboriginals and the tribes of New Guinea are the descendants of this first wave of Pacific settlers. The islands of Micronesia ('tiny islands') and Polynesia ('many islands') remained uninhabited until around five or six thousand years ago. At this time the Austronesian people of South-East Asia started to move beyond New Guinea to the islands which now comprise the Solomons, Vanuatu and Fiji.

The Austronesian language group includes the languages of South-East Asia (from Indonesian to Vietnamese) and the languages of the Pacific which developed as a sub-group as people moved into the Pacific. Around 1500 BC people moved on from Fiji to Tonga and this group is assumed to have included the ancestors of all the Polynesian people. Their language gradually diverged to become Polynesian as settlers moved to Samoa around 300 BC and to the Society Islands and Marquesas (now both part of French Polynesia) in the early years AD. The final great waves of Polynesian migration are thought to have taken place around 400 AD to Easter Island and between 500 and 800 AD to the other islands of modern French Polynesia, the Cook Islands and to New Zealand. Pukapuka in the Cooks, however, is thought to have been settled directly from Samoa or even earlier from Tonga.

It's uncertain exactly when the first settlers did reach the Cook Islands. Legends trace Rarotongan ancestry back about 600 years but early ceremonial adzes found on the islands are much older and the ancient Ara Metau road on Rarotonga is thought to be about 1000 years old. For the population to have grown to a size sufficient to construct such a major project it is assumed at least 500 years must have elapsed. Thus there may have been settlements on Rarotonga, and probably the other southern islands, for 1500 years.

Early Cook Islands Society

Rarotonga has always been the most important island of the Cooks and it's assumed the culture of its early inhabitants was largely duplicated on the on the other islands.

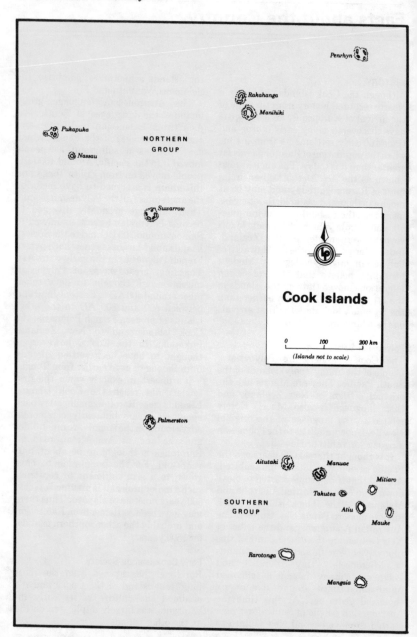

Pre-European Rarotonga was divided into districts headed by a hierarchy of chiefs the most important of whom was the *ariki*. The districts were divided into *tapere* populated by a related group known as *ngati* and headed by a lesser chief known as a *mataiapo*. *Tapere* were typically around 150 hectares in area and had a population of 100 to 200. Each *tapere* had its own ceremonial ground or *marae* which was used for both meetings and for religious purposes. The *koutu* was a similar centre at the district level.

Although in some respects this pattern of relationship and land ownership was firmly established in other ways it was quite flexible. The line of chieftainship for example, was not totally based on the male line and early European visitors gravely misunderstood the Rarotongan system by trying to translate what they observed into purely European terms. Hereditary titles could also be created and an *ariki* who became particularly powerful might have to create *rangatira* titles as a reward for his faithful supporters.

A chief's control over his people was related to his *mana*, a sort of supernatural power which he was felt to possess. A person's *mana* came not only from his birth but also from his achievements and status. *Mana* could not only be gained it could also be lost. An *ariki* who became unpopular (for example by interfering excessively in the distribution of crops) might suddenly find that his followers perceived a dramatic decline in his *mana*, which might even lead to him losing his control.

Control of *tapu* was a powerful weapon for an *ariki*. Certain activities were *tapu* or forbidden for supernatural reasons and since a chief could often decide what was or was not *tapu* this gave him considerable power. It was the people's strong belief in an *ariki's* combination of inherent *mana* and control of *tapu* which made the *ariki* so powerful and allowed them to exert control over their people without

necessarily having the physical means to exert their will. Unfortunately the early missionaries failed to fully understand the structure of the Rarotongan society and virtually ignored the operations of the pre-European religion.

The islands were not as extensively cultivated as the first missionaries' reports may have indicated and many crops were disastrously susceptible to the occasional severe hurricanes. A bad storm could completely destroy an island's crops and lead to terrible famines until replanting could be completed.

European Explorers

The Spanish explorers Alvaro de Mendana and Pedro Quiros were the first Europeans to sight islands in the group in 1595. They sailed through the northern group and stopped at Pukapuka. In his expeditions of 1773 and 1777 Captain James Cook explored much of the group although, remarkably, he never sighted the largest island, Rarotonga. That honour was left to the mutineers on *HMS Bounty* who touched upon Rarotonga in 1789. The mutiny actually took place after the *Bounty* sailed from Aitutaki. Those modern historians who place the blame for the famous event on the seductive qualities of Polynesian women, as opposed to Captain Bligh's cruelty, possibly had the Cook Islanders in mind! From Rarotonga the mutineers sailed on to Pitcairn Island in their search for a refuge where they would not be reached by the long arm of the British navy.

Cook, following what was virtually an English tradition of attaching truly terrible names to truly exotic places, dubbed the group the Hervey Islands. Later, a Russian cartographer renamed them, with an equal lack of inspiration, the Cook Islands. It was not until the islands were annexed by New Zealand that the whole southern and northern group were known by the one name.

Missionaries

Missionaries followed the explorers and the Reverend John Williams made his first appearance at the island of Aitutaki in 1821. He left two Polynesian 'teachers' behind and when he returned two years later they had made remarkable progress. Indeed the conversion of the Cook Islanders, generally accomplished in its initial stages by Polynesian converts, went far faster and more easily than it had done in the Society Islands, from where the missionaries generally came.

Papeiha, the most successful of these original missionaries, was moved to Rarotonga in 1823 and he laboured there for the rest of his life. In that period the missionaries totally swept across the islands and established a religious control which has held strong to this very day. They completely wiped out the original island religion and traditions and established what was virtually a religious police state. The height of their power was from 1835 to 1880 when their rigid and fiercely enforced laws were backed up by a system where fines on wrongdoers were split between the police and judges. Naturally this turned police work into an extremely lucrative profession and in parts of Rarotonga one person in every six was in the police force, ready and willing to turn in their neighbours for a cut in the proceeds. The missionary 'Blue Laws' included strict limitations on what you could do and where you could go on a Sunday, and there was even a law requiring any man who walked with an arm around a woman after dark to carry a light in his other hand!

The missionaries, although their influence was huge, left the actual government of the islands to the native chiefs or *ariki*. Therefore although Rarotonga, the headquarters for the London Missionary Society, became an important centre for the group it was not a government centre. The individual Cook Islands remained as separate and independent entities. Due to their relative isolation, small populations, lack of economic importance, and their generally poor harbour facilities the islands were largely neglected and ignored by traders, whalers and the European powers. The missionaries also worked hard at keeping other Europeans at arm's length.

Disease, Population Decline & Slavers

The missionaries intended to bring far

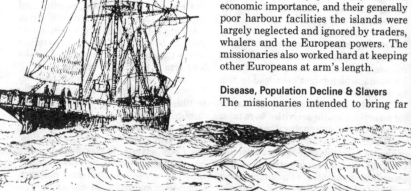

Mission ship *John Williams.*

more than just Christianity to the islands of Polynesia: they planned to bring peace, an end to cannibalism and infanticide and a general improvement in living standards. Unfortunately they also brought previously unknown diseases and destroyed the islanders' traditional culture. The consequences were a drastic and long lasting population decline. The poor Cook Islanders took the onslaught of deadly new diseases as a message from above to abandon their old religion and fall in with the new.

Undoubtedly the diseases would have soon arrived – courtesy of traders and whalers – whether or not the missionaries had brought them, but the statistics are nevertheless horrifying. When the missionaries first arrived in Rarotonga in 1823 the population was probably around 6000 to 7000 (it's around 10,000 today). The first major assault on this population was the arrival of dysentery, from Tahiti, in 1830. It killed nearly a thousand people in a single year. A whole series of European diseases from whooping cough to measles, smallpox and influenza followed. Each was new to the Cooks and each took a terrible toll.

Throughout the 19th century deaths exceeded births and by 1854, when an accurate census was finally taken, the population of Rarotonga was less than 2500, a decline of about two-thirds! By 1867 the population had dropped to 1856 and although migration from other islands began to create an artificial increase in the population of Rarotonga the decline in the group's total population did not start to level out until the late 19th century. It was not until early this century that a real increase in population began.

The trend of emigrating from the outer islands to Rarotonga that commenced in the 19th century continued, so that although the population decline on Rarotonga slowed it was only at the expense of a greater decline on other islands. Many islanders left for work on other Pacific islands, particularly Tahiti, but also on various plantation islands established by European traders. This migration continues to the present day as islanders move first to Rarotonga and then on to New Zealand or Australia.

Disease was not the only cause of the drop in population. The new housing designs introduced by the missionaries were damp and poorly ventilated and probably contributed to the death rate. In addition, a brutal Peruvian slave trade took a terrible toll on the islands of the northern group, although the trade lasted a mere seven months from late 1862 to 1863. At first the traders may have genuinely operated as labour recruiters but they quickly turned to subterfuge and outright kidnapping to round up their human cargoes. The Cook Islands were not the only ones visited by the traders but Tongareva was their very first port of call and it has been estimated that three-quarters of the population was taken. Rakahanga and Pukapuka were also victims of the slavers.

Few of the recruits, whether they went freely, as many did in the beginning, or through baser methods, ever returned to the islands. Over 90% either died in transit to Peru, died in Peru, or died while being repatriated. At the time of repatriation efforts Peru was suffering from a terrible smallpox epidemic and many Polynesians died from this while travelling back and, far worse, brought the disease back to their islands. One ship left Peru with 29 islanders and landed 15 smallpox-infected survivors on the island of Nukuviha (French Polynesia); the subsequent epidemic killed nearly a thousand people on Nukuviha and a further 500 on a neighbouring island.

The islanders' limited contact with westerners and the fact that what little contact they had experienced had been relatively benign was a major factor in why they were easy prey for the South Americans. As the missionary William Wyatt Gill commented:

Their simplicity of character, their kindness to visitors, their utter ignorance of the depths of depravity and deceit in the hearts of wicked white men, render them the easy dupes of designing characters.

Protectorate & Annexation

Despite their considerable influence via the missionaries the British did not formally take control of the Cook Islands until 1888. In that year the islands were declared a British protectorate by a Captain Bourke who arrived off Rarotonga in the warship *HMS Hyacinth*. To some extent this inevitable, although reluctant, extension of British control was due to fears that the French might decide to extend their power from neighbouring Tahiti in the Society Islands.

It's indicative of the hasty manner in which the British finally took over the islands that they failed to make a firm decision on just which islands would be included in the protectorate. The unfortunate Captain Bourke also managed to get the ceremony wrong and technically *annex* the islands rather than simply bring them under British protection! This caused some embarrassment and the process later had to be reversed in the southern islands where he had hoisted the flag, although for some reason Aitutaki remained annexed. One by one the others islands in the southern and northern groups were brought under British control.

The first British Resident, F J Moss, arrived in 1891 but his period in the islands was not a great success. In part this was due to his basic failure to understand the complexities of the *ariki* system, and the inappropriate application of European economic assumptions to a wholly different system. Moss was given the shove with some lack of ceremony in 1898 and the new Resident, W E Gudgeon, adopted a totally different method of running the islands. He ruled with an iron hand but his methods were also far from universally successful.

In the late 1890s the question of whether the islands should be associated with Britain or New Zealand was batted back and forth. Finally in 1900 Rarotonga and the other main southern islands were annexed to New Zealand and the net was widened to encompass all the southern and northern islands in 1901.

Population & Economics

A major problem facing the islands during the early years of British power was the steadily declining population. The combination of disease, slavery, and migration meant that the population of the islands had fallen to less than half the pre-contact level. Gudgeon, whose opinion of the islanders under his charge was far from complimentary, was convinced they were a dying race. Finally in the early part of this century the population started to slowly increase, although there were continuing migration losses, first to Tahiti and later to New Zealand.

Economics was another major problem and an answer to the islands' economic difficulties is still far away. Prior to their takeover the New Zealand government

Make Taukau, Queen of Rarotonga at annexation

was convinced that the Cooks could easily be made self-sufficient but this turned out to be a frequently repeated fallacy. The easy-going Polynesian nature, combined with shipping difficulties which continue to this day, defeated all attempts to tap the obvious agricultural richness of the islands, particularly the volcanic islands of the south.

The difficulty of improving the economic situation in the islands was felt by some officials to be related to the *ariki* system and land ownership patterns. Since land was traditionally controlled by the *ariki*, commoners did not have land to grow produce and the *ariki* often preferred to leave land unused rather than set a precedent for use by outsiders. The power of the *ariki* has gradually been weakened but they wield some influence even today and the land ownership system is still a major disincentive to improving the use of agricultural land.

Independence

During WW II the USA built airstrips on Penrhyn and Aitutaki, but the Cooks remained a quietly forgotten New Zealand dependency. In the 1960s it was belatedly realised that colonies were becoming an aberration and the path to independence was plotted with considerable haste. In 1965 the Cook Islands became internally self-governing but foreign policy and defence were left to New Zealand. The continuing problem of the population drain accelerated after independence.

The close links with New Zealand have precluded the Cook Islands from taking a seat in the United Nations, and it has to be admitted that a country with a population of less than 20,000 is bound to face considerable difficulties in achieving real self-sufficiency in the modern world. The Cook Islanders derive a number of benefits from their semi-independence from New Zealand including New Zealand citizenship and the right to come and go from New Zealand at will. Not only is the population of Cook Islanders in New Zealand actually greater than in the islands themselves but it's also a very important source of income for the nation.

Elections in 1968 brought Albert Henry, leader of the Cook Islands Party and a prime mover in the push for independence, to power. In 1972 he was once again elected prime minister and he later became Sir Albert Henry. Sir Albert was an Aitutakian and it's said that the people of this island are such keen arguers and debaters that they'll get themselves into trouble simply for the joy of talking their way out of it. With the 1978 elections Sir Albert got himself into deep trouble.

The problem revolved around the great number of Cook Islanders living overseas, principally in New Zealand. Sir Albert feared that the forthcoming election was going to be a close one and dreamt up the ingenious plan of organising a series of charter flights from Auckland, New Zealand to Rarotonga, bringing back hordes of Cook Islanders for a short vacation and a quick visit to the polling booths – where they would gratefully vote for the provider of their free tickets. It worked a treat: 445 Cook Islanders were flown back by the Australian airline Ansett at a cost of $290,000 and Sir Albert was duly re-elected.

Then came the protests of electoral fraud, a High Court case followed and eventually Sir Albert was kicked out of office by the Chief Justice. In 1980 he was stripped of his knighthood and in early 1981 he died, some say broken-hearted. You can see his grave in the CICC church graveyard in Avarua.

A truly multi-dimensional man, Dr Tom Davis, leader of the Democratic Party, was the new Prime Minister. Before returning to the Cook Islands to enter politics he'd qualified as a doctor in New Zealand, become Chief Medical Officer to the islands, written a book titled *Doctor to the Islands*, studied in Australia, sailed a yacht to the US and studied at Harvard, and become an expert on space medicine with NASA.

In the next election in 1983, however, the Democratic Party was bundled out and another Henry took over as Prime Minister. Dr Davis had become Sir Thomas Davis during his period in power

but in the 1983 election he even lost his seat in parliament. Unfortunately for the new leader, Geoffrey Henry, a cousin of Albert Henry, politics in the Cook Islands is a family affair and his family quickly turned against him. When two other important Henrys withdrew their support Geoffrey Henry soon found he'd lost his parliamentary majority. Parliament was dissolved, a new election was called and this time round the Democratic Party squeezed back in with Sir Thomas Davis once more Prime Minister. In his own electorate Sir Thomas' majority was just five votes.

Politics may be colourful but the Cook Islands are generally quite stable. The government's biggest problem is simply managing the economy and trying to keep some sort of balance between the meagre exports and the avalanche of imports.

GOVERNMENT

The Cook Islands have a Westminster parliamentary system of government like that of England, Australia or New Zealand. Of course with a population of 20,000 it's on a small scale and the Cook Islands Parliament inhabits an inconspicuous building beside the Rarotonga airport. The Prime Minister has his office on top of the Post Office in Avarua and across the road is a parking space marked 'Prime Minister' for his '85 Jaguar XJ6, bought second-hand in Sydney in 1986.

The Parliament has two houses. The lower house or Legislative Assembly has 24 elected members. The upper house or House of Ariki represents the island chiefs but they have only advisory powers.

Away from Rarotonga each island has an appointed Chief Administrative Officer or CAO. This is a direct carry over from the Resident Agent of colonial times and indeed the CAO's house on each island is still known as The Residency. The CAO generally has more power than the elected Island Council.

Top: The Banana Court Bar, Rarotonga – one of the best bars in the Pacific (TW)
Left: 'Island Night' at the Rapae Hotel, Aitutaki (TW)
Right: Dancer, Rarotonga (CITA)

ECONOMY

The Cook Islands' economy is far from balanced – there are much fewer exports than imports. The biggest factor in making up the shortfall is good old foreign aid, particularly from big-brother New Zealand. Considerable amounts of money are also sent back by Cook Islanders living abroad – remember there are more Cook Islanders living abroad than are actually in the Cooks.

Exports are almost totally dependent on New Zealand so if the Kiwis sneeze the Cook Islanders catch a cold. New Zealand is a small market and for the Cooks it has sometimes been a fickle one. The biggest export category is clothing and footwear which enjoys privileged entry in New Zealand. Next up comes fresh fruit and vegetables. Citrus fruit is the major agricultural export although pineapples (from Atiu), other tropical fruits such as bananas and papayas (pawpaw) and vegetables such as beans, tomatoes, capsicums (bell peppers) and zucchini (courgettes) are also exported. Much of this produce is airfreighted out; an important plus for tourism is that agriculture creates an additional demand for aircraft. The inevitable copra, produced throughout the Pacific, is another important export and there is also a continuing supply of pearl shell.

The most important money earner for the Cooks, however, is tourism. It's number one and growing faster than anything else. Other important money earners include the Cook Islands' beautiful and cleverly marketed postage stamps and the status of the islands as a tax haven.

For the casual visitor it's very hard to get any sort of handle on the economy of the Cooks, or more particularly of Rarotonga. On one hand the balance of trade is undoubtedly pretty horrific and the Cook Islanders live far beyond their means. On the other hand everybody is undeniably well fed. It's a popular joke that when *Merry Christmas Mr Lawrence* (a WW II prison camp drama starring David Bowie) was filmed in Rarotonga it proved impossible to find 500 people who looked thin enough to appear as prison camp extras. Extras had to be flown in from New Zealand.

In fact the excess of food is appalling – food simply drops on the ground and rots. The fat 'plop' of breadfruit landing on the road is a familiar sound to anybody strolling around Rarotonga. Avocadoes grow in such profusion that they are chiefly used as pig food. Exotic tropical fruits litter the ground around trees all over the island. It's a wasteful and saddening sight but, in part at least, it can't be blamed on the Cook Islanders – it's simply too difficult and too expensive to get this excess produce to market and the market (New Zealand) is too small to absorb it in any case.

What is surprising, given this agricultural excess, is how bloody expensive things are. If there's so much produce that it falls to the ground because it's not worth picking how come vegetables are five times more expensive than they are in Australia? Even oranges, the one really important export crop, are much more expensive. Why is the market in Avarua such a pale shadow of the colourful, packed, bustling markets of other countries? Why are the supermarkets packed with imported fruit juice from New Zealand when they produce excellent fruit juice right here in Rarotonga? It's true many of the supermarket shoppers are island visitors but not every local resident grows their own produce. And let's not even think about the ultimate obscenity: canned fish on a Pacific island.

Perhaps from the point of view of a western work ethic, living in Rarotonga is simply too easy. The climate and the soil is of a type where any stick shoved into the ground is a tree by next week and bearing fruit by the week after. Islanders comment how a couple of months work a year provides all the food they could possibly eat and the hardest work they have to do is getting their export produce to the airport on Saturday mornings. Yet the outside world beckons beyond this easy life; alcohol is a major problem with the younger people and the population drain to the bright lights of Auckland continues unabated.

Land Ownership

The Cook Islands' land ownership policy has a great influence on the islands' economy and its social patterns. A law makes it impossible for outsiders to own land in the Cooks by prohibiting anybody from selling or buying land. Land ownership is purely hereditary and land can only be leased to an outside party. As usual with any such arrangement it's a two-edged sword.

The plus side is that there has been no invasion by the outside world. No international hotel groups have bought up the coastline of Rarotonga and international jet-setters haven't grabbed land all over the islands for holiday homes. But on the other hand there are no large and efficient agricultural operations which might have encouraged exports and helped solve the problems which lead to such an awesome proportion of Rarotonga's agricultural output simply rotting. Nor is anybody very keen on spending money or effort on improvements to land or buildings. Why bother? You can't sell it to anybody and if your children have all moved abroad there's nobody to even leave it to. There are a surprising number of derelict houses around the islands.

The land ownership policy has its amusing consequences as well. Because land is passed from generation to generation but never sold to outsiders people start to own curiously divided chunks of property. Many families seem to have a house by the coast, a citrus plantation somewhere else, a taro patch somewhere else again and the odd group of papaya trees dotted here and there. It can be a full time job commuting from one farmlet to another.

Today the houses you see around the islands are almost all cheaply made imitation-European-style with fibro walls and tin roofs. Very few of the old *kikau* houses with their roofs thatched with pandanus remain.

PEOPLE

In the 1981 census the population of the Cook Islands was 17,227. There's at least that number again outside the Cook Islands, most of them in New Zealand where Cook Islanders have residence rights. The story of the Cook Islands' population is a story of continuing movement from the outer islands to Rarotonga and from there to New Zealand.

Over 90% of the population lives on the southern islands. None of the lightly populated atolls of the northern group have a four figure population. Population estimates are:

island	group	population
Rarotonga	southern	9300
Aitutaki	southern	2400
Mangaia	southern	1530
Atiu	southern	1300
Pukapuka	northern	780
Mauke	southern	700
Penrhyn	northern	530
Mitiaro	southern	300
Rakahanga	northern	280
Manihiki	northern	260
Nassau	northern	110
Palmerston	northern	50

There are a number of unpopulated islands in both the northern and southern groups.

The population is over 90% Polynesian – closely related to the Maoris of New Zealand. Maoris and Cook Islanders even speak basically the same language and the Cook Islanders relate stories of how they set out to populate New Zealand from Rarotonga. There are small minorities of Europeans, principally New Zealanders, and Chinese.

There are often subtle differences between the islands, in some cases due to their isolation. The people of Pukapuka in the north, for example, are in some ways more closely related to Samoa than to the other islands of the group; geographically the northern Cook Islands are closer to Samoa than they are to the southern Cook Islands.

LANGUAGE

The language of the Cook Islands is Cook

Islands Maori or Rarotongan but English is very widely spoken, usually with a broad New Zealand accent, and you will have no trouble at all getting by with English.

Learning a few words and phrases of Maori can be fun; try the following:

kia orana – all purpose greeting, literally 'may you live'

aere ra – goodbye, literally 'go along'

kia manuia – good luck (a toast)

ae – yes

kare – no

meitaki – thankyou or good

Maori – Polynesian person, the local language, anything local – *tiare Maori* means a local flower

Papa'a – westerner, also English language

tane – man

vaine – woman

If you want to look learn some more Maori pick up a copy of *Say it in Rarotongan* (Mana Strickland, Pacific Publications, Sydney) which is widely available in the Cook Islands. Although there are minor variations between the islands the language is virtually the same everywhere. Cook Islands Maori is also very closely related to the Maori language of New Zealand and to the other eastern Polynesian languages including Hawaiian, Marquesan and Tahitian. A Cook Islander would have no trouble understanding someone speaking those languages. Cook Islands Maori, in its Rarotongan form, was first written down by the missionaries in the 1830s. Later they produced a Rarotongan version of the Bible.

Names

To our ears the Cook Islanders have some pretty strange given names. There's no differentiation between male or female names and they're often given to commemorate some event that happened around the time the name's recipient was born. Big brother just left your island to go off to school on another island? Well you might end up as 'Schooltrip'.

The school was far away in Whangarei, New Zealand? You could be named 'Whangarei'. Big brother won a medal in the Commonwealth Games? You're 'Silver Medal'! But why would somebody be named 'Tipuni' or 'Teaspoon'? And why are there so many people named 'Unlucky'?

RELIGION

Remarkably little is known about the pre-European religion of the Cook Islands. The early missionaries held 'pagan beliefs' in such utter contempt that they made virtually no effort to study, record or understand it. They did, however, make great efforts to wipe it out and destroy any heathen images they came across. Fortunately some fine pieces of religious art were whisked away from the islands and are now prized pieces in European museums.

The Cook Islands today are overwhelmingly Christian – in fact people from Christian cultures who haven't been

Tangaroa

to church (weddings and funerals apart) for years suddenly find themselves going back to church for fun! The major local sect is the Cook Islands Christian Church or CICC. An offspring of those first British missionaries in 1821 it's a blend of Church of England, Baptist, Methodist and whatever else was going down at the time – Roman Catholicism definitely excepted. Today the CICC still attracts 60% of the faithful, in Rarotonga at least. The remaining 40% is squabbled over by the Roman Catholics, the Seventh Day Adventists, the Church of the Latter Day Saints (Mormons looking as out of place in their white shirts and ties as ever) and various other sects.

The CICC still has an overwhelming influence on local living habits and in many cases the pattern is exactly that established by those original British missionaries a century and a half ago. Rarotongan villages are still divided into four sections which take turn-about in looking after the village church and its minister. Each family in the congregation pays NZ$6 a month into the church fund which goes towards church costs. The church minister is appointed for a five year period after which he moves to another church. He gets a weekly stipend of NZ$15 (and a bunch of bananas) but in addition the village group responsible for that week also collects to provide him with a more reasonable weekly salary. The weekly contribution is read out during the Sunday service to the shame or pride of that week's responsible group!

This village responsibility has two sides for the church minister. He is responsible for far more than just his church: if the village teenagers are playing up or hanging around the local bars the blame is likely to be laid at the CICC minister's door! And if he doesn't do something about it then a pitifully low weekly contribution can be interpreted as a strong hint to get on with the job. In fact islanders say that they prefer to have a minister with no local connections –

someone from an outer island, say. That way if they decide to kick him out by cutting the money supply he's not going to find it so easy to fall back on the food from his local gardens!

Visitors are more than welcome to attend a Sunday church service and it's a delightful event to visit. You're looked upon as a useful way of augmenting the collection and anyway there's nothing much else happening on a Sunday. The service is held in Maori although there may be a token welcome in English in tourist-popular churches like the CICC in Arorangi. The major attraction is the inspired hymn singing – the harmonies are terrific and the volume lifts the roof. The islanders all dress in their Sunday best and the women all wear strikingly similar wide-brimmed hats.

Early Missionaries

Important figures in the early spread of Christianity through the islands included:

Aaron Buzacott Following in John Williams footsteps Buzacott not only did most of the work in translating the Bible into Maori, he also composed most of the hymns in the CICC Maori hymn book. Buzacott also supervised the construction of the church in Avarua, Rarotonga and died in 1864 after 30 years work in the Cook Islands.

William Gill Author of *Gems from the Coral Island* William Gill built the present CICC church at Arorangi, Rarotonga and also its predecessor, destroyed by a hurricane in 1846. He worked at Arorangi from 1839 to 1852 when he returned to England. His brother George Gill was the first resident missionary on Mangaia.

William Wyatt Gill Author of *From Darkness to Light in Polynesia* William Wyatt Gill was no relation to William Gill. He spent 20 years on Mangaia – see the Books section for more details.

Maretu Maretu's accounts (see the Books section) of the spread of Christianity are particularly interesting because they are by a Cook Islander rather than a European. A native of Rarotonga, Maretu later worked as a missionary on Mangaia, Manihiki and Rakahanga.

Papeiha Probably the most successful of the local mission workers Papeiha was brought from Raiatea in the Society Islands and introduced Christianity to Aitutaki in 1821 and to Rarotonga in 1823. He died in Rarotonga in 1867 having spent 46 years in the Cook Islands.

John Williams A pioneer mission worker in the Pacific he was instrumental in the spread of Christianity to the Cook Islands. He was killed (and eaten) on the New Hebrides island of Eromanga in 1839.

DANCING

Dancing in the Cook Islands is colourful, spectacular and popular. The Cook Islanders are reputed to be the best dancers in Polynesia, even better than the Tahitians say the connoisseurs. You'll get plenty of opportunity to see dancing as there are dances on all the time, particularly at the ubiquitous 'island nights'. Entry charges to see the dances are often only a dollar or two or simply the price of a drink.

The dancing is often wonderfully suggestive and, hardly surprisingly, this caused some upset to the Victorian European visitors. You can almost feel William Wyatt Gill, the observant early missionary, raising his eyebrows as he reported that:

Respecting the *morality* of their dances, the less said the better; but the 'upaupa' dance, introduced from Tahiti, is obscene indeed.

Things haven't changed much!

If you go to the annual dance championships in Rarotonga the points which judges watch for will probably be outlined. They include the difficulty of the dance, the movements of the hands which must express the music, the facial expressions and the grace with which the dance is done. Male dances tend to be aggressive and energetic, female dances are often all languid suggestiveness and gyrating hips. It's a lot of fun. Don't concentrate solely on the dancers – the musicians are wonderful to watch and the audience often gets involved in a big way. Some of the fat mamas are simply superb and, despite their weight, can shake a hip as well as any young *vaine*. Take note of how it's done though; a feature of almost every island night is dragging an unsuspecting *papa'a* on stage to perform!

Of course western ideals of beauty have gained considerable ascendancy these days and it's only as they get older that some Polynesian women start to widen so dramatically. In the missionary period William Wyatt Gill wrote:

The greatest requisite of a Polynesian beauty is to be fat and as fair as their dusky skin will permit. To insure this, favourite children in good families, whether boys or girls, were regularly fattened and imprisoned till nightfall, when a little gentle exercise was permitted. If refractory, the guardian would even whip the culprit for not eating more, calling out 'Shall I not be put to shame to see you so slim in the dance?'

FESTIVALS & HOLIDAYS

There are lots of holidays in the Cook Islands and they're good opportunities to see dancing and other activities. The two major sports in the Cooks are rugby, which is played with all-out passion from May to August, and cricket, over the summer months, particularly December to March.

New Year's Day 1 January is a public holiday and there is horse racing at Muri Beach.

Cultural Festival Week In the third week of

February, this week is marked by canoe races and arts and crafts displays.

Island Dance Festival Week In the second week of April dance displays and competitions include the important individual Dancers of the Year Competition.

Anzac Day (public holiday) As in New Zealand and Australia 25 April is an annual memorial day for the soldiers of the two world wars.

Good Friday & Easter Monday The two principal easter days are both public holidays. On Easter Monday there is horse racing at Muri Beach.

Queen's Birthday As in New Zealand and Australia the Queen's 'official' birthday is a public holiday.

Constitution Celebration This 10-day festival starts on the Friday before 4 August and celebrates independence on 4 August 1965 with sporting activities and other events. This is the major festival of the year

Cook Islands Art Exhibition Week Second week in September.

Cook Islands Fashion Week Third week in October.

Gospel Day (public holiday) The raising of the British flag over Rarotonga on 26 October 1888 by Captain Bourke of *HMS Hyacinth* is celebrated on this day. *Nuku* religious plays are performed.

Round Rarotonga Run This popular early November fun run circles the island on the coast road. The record for the 32 km distance is just over 98 minutes.

Tiare (floral) Festival Week In the third week in November with tiare float parades and flower arranging competitions.

Christmas Day (public holiday) 25 December is celebrated with church services.

Boxing Day 26 December is also a public holiday and there is horse racing at Muri Beach.

New Year's Eve The new year is welcomed with dancing and other entertainment.

GEOGRAPHY

The Cook Islands have a total land area of just 241 square km – that's about a quarter of the area of the Australian Capital Territory or of Rhode Island (the smallest USA state). This inconspicuous land mass is scattered over about two million square km of sea, an area as large as western Europe. The islands are south of the equator, slightly east of the International Date Line and about midway between American Samoa and Tahiti. Rarotonga is 1260 km from Tahiti and 3447 km from Auckland, New Zealand.

The 15 islands are conveniently divided into northern and southern groups, separated by as much as 1000 km of empty sea. The islands are:

Southern Group

island	land area (square km)	type
Rarotonga	67.2	high volcanic
Mangaia	51.8	raised atoll
Atiu	26.9	raised atoll
Mitiaro	22.3	raised atoll
Mauke	18.4	raised atoll
Aitutaki	18.1	high volcanic & lagoon atoll
Manuae*	~6.2	coral lagoon atoll
Palmerston	2.0	coral lagoon atoll
Takutea*	1.2	low coral atoll

Northern Group

Penrhyn	~9.8	coral lagoon atoll

Manihiki	9.8	coral lagoon atoll
Pukapuka	5.1	coral lagoon atoll
Rakahanga	4.1	coral lagoon atoll
Nassau	1.2	low coral atoll
Suwarrow*	0.4	coral lagoon atoll

* unpopulated

There are some clear differences between the two groups quite apart from their geographical separation. The southern islands are generally larger, more heavily populated, economically better off and more closely connected with the outside world. They're actually a continuation of the Austral Islands in the south of French Polynesia. They lie along the same north-west to south-east fracture in the earth's crust. The southern islands are also volcanic, mountainous islands while the northern islands are coral atolls. The southern islands make up about 90% of the total land area of the whole Cook Islands.

That simplistic definition of high volcanic islands in the south versus atolls in the north can be further refined. Only Rarotonga, which is the youngest island in the group, is a straightforward volcanic, mountainous island like Tahiti in French Polynesia. Aitutaki is mountainous, but also has a surrounding atoll reef like Bora Bora in French Polynesia.

Four of the southern group – Atiu, Mangaia, Mauke and Mitiaro – are raised atolls. They have been raised up from the ocean floor at some time in the past and their fringing reef has become a rocky coastal area known as a *makatea*, surrounding a central region of volcanic soil. In Atiu and Mangaia the *makatea* surrounds a hilly central plateau while Mauke and Mitiaro are virtually flat with a swampy central region. Two of the southern group are uninhabited and very small while Palmerston is a coral atoll like the northern group, and indeed is

sometimes included with the northern group.

All the northern group are coral atolls and most take the classic Pacific form with an outer reef encircling a lagoon and small islands dotting this reef. An atoll of this type is basically a submerged volcano – only the outer rim of the volcano breaks the surface of the sea and this is where the reef and islands are. The lagoon in the centre is the volcano crater. All the northern islands except Penrhyn rise from the Manihiki Plateau, an area of the ocean bottom 3000 metres deep. Penrhyn rises from west of this platform where the ocean is 5000 metres deep. The Penrhyn volcano is thus much 'higher' than the other northern islands. Nassau is unique in the northern group because it is simply a single island with an encircling reef – not a group of islands around a lagoon. All the northern atolls are very low – waves can wash right over them in hurricanes and you have to be very close in order to see them from a ship.

FLORA & FAUNA

In common with most other Pacific islands the fauna is limited. The only native mammals are rats (which reach plague proportions on many islands) and bats. Pigs were introduced at some early stage, however. Today many of them run wild and cause a great deal of damage. There are many domestic pigs which are usually kept by the simple method of tying one leg to a coconut tree. Not unexpectedly they frequently escape. There are also a great number of dogs on Rarotonga and limited numbers of goats, horses and cattle.

Birds are more plentiful although the number of land birds is very limited and they have been considerably squeezed by the iniquitous mynah bird. Introduced from India, supposedly to eat wasps or hornets or something, the mynah found life in the Cook Islands so cushy that it didn't need to bother about doing what it was originally brought in for. Today the mynah is found in great numbers on most islands and has considerably reduced the number of native birds. In Rarotonga in particular you have to go up into the inland hills to find native birds.

Despite the limited number of birds there are some of great interest to birdwatchers including a surprising number of endemic birds – birds found only in the one localised area. Birds of particular interest include the cave-dwelling Atiu swiftlet on the island of Atiu, the chattering kingfisher of Atiu and Mauke and the Mangaia kingfisher of Mangaia. For more information pick up a copy of the booklet *Guide to Cook Islands Birds* by D T Holyoak (Cook Islands Library & Museum, Rarotonga, 1980).

Of course there are many fish in the waters around the islands. Fortunately for divers, sharks are not a problem. The islands of the southern group generally have such shallow lagoons that sharks and other large fish are usually found only outside the reef. Outside the reef, however, the drop-offs are often very steep and there are wonderful opportunities for scuba divers.

There are some other creatures you're likely to come across in the Cooks. Around Rarotonga, on the sandy lagoon bottom of Aitutaki and on other islands there are great numbers of sea slugs, also known as *beche de mer* or in Maori as *pirau*. Certain varieties of these strange sausage-like creatures are a noted delicacy. Bright-blue starfish are also a common sight. On land as well as in the water the Cooks have a great number of crabs – ranging from amusing hermit crabs to large coconut crabs.

The island flora varies widely from island to island. The two most noticeable features are probably the coconut palm and the great variety of flowers which seem to grow with wild abandon almost everywhere. On the atolls of the northern group the soil is usually limited and infertile and there is little vegetation apart from the coconut palms. Rarotonga has a wide variety of vegetation. The damp, mountainous central part of the island is densely covered in a luxuriant jungle with ferns, creepers and towering trees.

The raised atoll islands of the southern group such as Mangaia or Atiu are particularly interesting for the sharp dividing line between the fertile central area with volcanic soil, the swampy transition zone between the fossil coral *makatea* and the central region and the wild vegetation on the *makatea* itself. Although the *makatea* is described as rocky and infertile it's actually covered with amazingly lush growth, although the actual range of vegetation that can survive in this inhospitable region is very limited.

VISAS

For most nationalities no visa is required and a 31-day stay is granted on arrival. This can usually be extended at the immigration department in Avarua. If you are intending to visit the northern islands (and not continue through to Samoa) it's wise to extend your permit before heading up as there are often delays. The only requirements for visitors are the loosely policed 'prior booking' arrangement (see Accommodation) and the fact that your airline tickets out of the country are checked on arrival. Presumably if you intended to depart the Cook Islands by the infrequent shipping service through to Samoa you would have to do some fast talking at the airport and, most probably, provide proof of your financial stability.

If you want to stay longer than the initial 31 days you should have no problems so long as you can show you've got adequate finances and still have your vital ticket out. Each one-month extension costs NZ$20 and must be applied for 14 days before the expiry of your current permit. You're allowed three one-month extensions to take you to a total of four months. If you want to stay more than four months you're supposed to apply from abroad to either the Principal Immigration Officer, Ministry of Labour & Commerce in Rarotonga; to the Cook Islands Government Office in Auckland; or to a New Zealand diplomatic office. The major problem with long term visits to the Cooks is finding a place to live. No land can be bought or sold and land or property for lease is hard to find, despite the many empty or even derelict houses on the islands.

MONEY

The Cook Islands use New Zealand currency which currently exchanges at:

US$1	= NZ$1.90	NZ$1	= US$053
A$1	= NZ$1.29	NZ$1	= A$0.78
£1	= NZ$2.80	NZ$1	= £0.36

You get about 4% more for travellers' cheques than for cash. There are not many places you can change money – the Bank of New Zealand in Avarua, the branch bank in Arorangi, the Post Office in Aitutaki, and some hotels. You're better off changing all your money in Rarotonga rather than hoping to be able to change money on the outer islands.

All Cook Islands prices in this book are quoted in NZ$ since the only Cook Islands dollar you're going to see is the one dollar coin. New Zealand paper money is used exclusively but there is also a complete set of Cook Islands coins – 1c, 2c, 5c, 10c, 20c, 50c and $1. Except for the huge Cook Islands dollar coin they're exactly the same size and shape as the New Zealand coins (and Australian ones for that matter) so you can use New Zealand coins for pay phones or other such uses quite easily. In fact you don't actually see Cook Islands coins in circulation very much; they're mainly collectors' items, particularly the $1 coin with its engraving of Tangaroa, a noted fertility symbol.

Credit Cards

Bankcard, the standard credit card in Australia and New Zealand, is readily accepted at most places in Rarotonga. Visa and Mastercard are also widely accepted; American Express and Diners Club are accepted at the better hotels and restaurants. Some places have signs indicating they accept all and sundry cards but when it comes to the crunch good old Bankcard is all they want to see.

Tipping & Bargaining

Don't. Tipping doesn't exist in the Cook Islands and a price is a price, don't expect to get it lowered.

COSTS

There's no way round it, the Cooks are expensive. Fortunately, while they are more expensive than Fiji they're not quite at the horrendous levels of Tahiti and French Polynesia. The New Zealand connection is both a factor for and against the steep costs. The Cook Islands are heavily dependent upon New Zealand for their imports so there's a healthy slug on top of New Zealand prices to cover the shipping costs. Shipping is a major element in the high prices of most Pacific islands. Additionally, and again like many other Pacific islands, there's a sad lack of self-sufficiency. It's a major disappointment to see the cans of mackerel and tuna in every trade store when the reef abounds with fish. Similarly, Rarotonga is extravagantly fertile but, oranges and some other fruit apart, much fruit and produce is imported at high cost. Even eggs are imported from New Zealand although chickens run underfoot in every village. See the Food section below for some suggestions on cutting the food costs.

The plus point about the Cook Islands' strong links to New Zealand is that for a number of years the New Zealand dollar has not been the world's strongest currency. So if the New Zealand dollar sinks relative to your home market currency (lucky Americans whose dollar buys almost two of the New Zealand variety) then prices in the Cook Islands also translate into that much less.

Another factor which can help to cut costs is that there is some cheaper accommodation although camping out is frowned upon. Most importantly, nearly all accommodation offers opportunities for preparing your own food at a substantial saving to eating out. See the Accommodation and Food sections for details.

Many visitors to the Cooks come on all-inclusive package holidays. There are many brochures available on these tours and land costs vary widely depending on the place you stay and whether or not meals or further travel are included.

CLIMATE

Rarotonga, the largest and most important of the Cook Islands, is virtually directly south of Hawaii and about the same distance south of the equator as Hawaii is north. The climate is therefore very similar to that of Hawaii although the seasons are reversed: December is the middle of summer, August the middle of winter.

The Cooks have a pleasantly even climate year round with no excesses of temperature, humidity or rainfall although it can rain quite often. Rarotonga, with its high mountains, is particularly likely to be wet and although you'd have to be unlucky to suffer one of the rare week-long rainy periods an umbrella is not a bad thing to take with you. The wettest months are usually December through March when around 25 cm of rain can fall each month. These are also the hottest months although the seasonal variation is very slight.

Despite the relatively heavy annual rainfall some of the islands, particularly the atolls of the northern group, suffer from severe water shortages and great care must be taken to conserve water.

Hurricanes usually come in the summer season from November to March. On average there's a hurricane two or three times a decade but extremely severe hurricanes are a much rarer occurrence.

BOOKS & BOOKSHOPS

There have been a surprising number of books written about the Cooks or in which the Cooks make at least an appearance. Unfortunately some of the most interesting are out of print and you will have to search libraries or second-hand bookshops if you want to find them. There are a number of unusual books actually available in the Cook Islands – in Rarotonga try the Bounty Bookshop, Island Crafts, Cook Islands Trading Company or the Library. All have a selection of books you'd be lucky to find elsewhere.

History

Alphons M J Kloosterman's *Discoverers of the Cook Islands & the Names they Gave* (Cook Islands Library & Museum, Rarotonga, 1976) gives a brief history of each island, the early legends relating to that island and a record of its European contact. It makes interesting reading and there's an exhaustive listing of the early descriptions of the islands by European visitors.

The Cook Islands, 1820-1950 by Richard Gilson (Victoria University Press, Wellington, 1980) is a rather starchy and dry history of the Cooks. There is an introductory chapter on the pre-European history of the islands but basically it relates the story from soon after the first missionary contact up until just after WW II. It concentrates heavily on boring descriptions of the economics and politics of the Cook Islands since annexation by New Zealand. It's also almost exclusively a Rarotongan history; little mention is made of the other islands in the group.

The Gospel Comes to Rarotonga by Taira Rere (Rarotonga, 1980) is a concise, locally written account of the arrival of

Christianity in the Cook Islands, particularly in Rarotonga. There are interesting thumbnail sketches of the various important participants in this chapter of the islands' history.

H E Maude's *Slavers in Paradise* (Australian National University, Canberra & Stanford University Press, Stanford, 1981) provides a readable yet detailed analysis of the Peruvian slave trade which wreaked havoc in Polynesia between 1862 and 1864. Some of the northern atolls were particularly badly hit by this cruel and inhumane trade. This book is available in the Cook Islands as a paperback from the University of the South Pacific (Suva, Fiji, 1986).

Missionaries' Accounts

The Reverend William Gill turned up in Rarotonga in 1839 and lived in the Cooks for the next 30 years. His book *Gems of the Coral Islands* (1858) is perceptive but heavily slanted towards the missionary view of life. The Cooks had a second William Gill: William *Wyatt* Gill was no relation at all to the other William Gill (he was only 11 years old when the older Gill started his missionary career) but he lived on the island of Mangaia for 20 years from 1852 and wrote several important studies. *From Darkness to Light in Polynesia* was originally published in 1894 but has recently been reissued in a University of the South Pacific paperback (Samoa, 1984).

In amongst these reports on the Cook Islands by outsiders there is also one interesting insider's point of view. The author, Maretu, was born in the Ngatangiia area of Rarotonga sometime around 1802. He was an older child when Europeans first visited Rarotonga in 1814 and a young man when the missionaries first arrived in 1823. Maretu later became a missionary himself and worked on several other islands in the group. In 1871 he sat down to write, in Rarotongan Maori, an account of the extraordinary events he had witnessed during his lifetime. Translated into English and extensively annotated, his illuminating work has been published as *Cannibals & Converts* (University of the South Pacific, 1983).

Residents' Accounts

A number of Cook Islands residents have gone into print with their tales of life in the South Pacific. Unfortunately very few of them are currently in print.

Robert Dean Frisbie's book *Island of Desire* is rated by some critics as a classic of South Pacific life. Frisbie was born in the USA and ran a store on Pukapuka; his eldest daughter Johnny also wrote of the Cook Islands in *The Frisbies of the South Seas*.

One of the best known resident writers would have to be Tom Neale, who wrote of his life as the hermit of Suwarrow in *An Island to Oneself* (Holt, Rinehart & Winston, New York, 1966 and Avon paperback). It's now out of print. Tom Neale lived by himself on the beautiful but totally isolated northern atoll of Suwarrow for a total of six years in two three-year spells in the late '50s and early '60s; his book recounts this period. He then returned to Suwarrow and lived there for most of the '70s until he was brought back to Rarotonga shortly before his death in 1977. Many Rarotongan residents have anecdotes to relate about Tom Neale or opinions of him and it seems that his book, which was actually ghost written, makes him out to be a much more reasonable fellow than he actually was. One person's opinion was that he was so cantankerous an uninhabited island was the only place for him. See the Suwarrow section for more details.

Isles of the Frigate Bird (Michael Joseph, London, 1975) and *The Lagoon is Lonely Now* (Millwood Press, Wellington, 1978) are both by Rarotongan resident Ronald Syme. The first book is mainly autobiographical and relates how the author came to the Cook Islands in the

early '50s and eventually settled down. Before finally ending up on Rarotonga he spent some time travelling around the islands and also lived on Mangaia for a while. The second book is more anecdotal, relating legends, customs and incidents of island life. It becomes a little tiresome at times with its constant reiteration of how much better things were in the 'old days' and how much better things could be if progress wasn't forced down the islanders' throats. Nevertheless both books make interesting reading and a good introduction to life in the Cook Islands, particularly during the period of great changes in the years since WW II.

There are countless earlier accounts of life in the Cooks, few of them currently available. F J Moss, for example, wrote of the islands in 1888 in his book *Through Atolls & Islands*. Julian Dashwood (*Rakau* or 'wood' in Maori) was a long running islands character and wrote two books about the Cooks. *I Know an Island* was published in the 1930s and he followed that with a second book in the '60s published as *Today is Forever* in the USA and as *Island Paradise* in England. *Sisters in the Sun* by A S Helm and W H Percival (Robert Hale, London, 1973) tells of Suwarrow and Palmerston.

The Cook Islands' Prime Minister, Sir Tom Davis, has also written a book of his time as a doctor on the islands, *Doctor to the Islands*.

Travellers' Accounts & Guidebooks

Across the South Pacific by Iain Finlay & Trish Shepherd (Angus & Robertson, Sydney, 1981) is an account of a trans-Pacific jaunt by a family of four. The Cook Islands section is particularly interesting for its description of taking the *Mataora* from Rarotonga through the northern group and across to Western Samoa. If you're considering island-hopping through the Cooks on a local freighter read this first!

How to Get Lost & Found in the Cook Islands by John W McDermott (Waikiki

Cook Islands News

25c

MONDAY 19 MAY 1986   PH 29460 RAROTONGA

Aitutaki Land

Publishing, Honolulu, 1979) is another in the Air New Zealand funded series by a Hawaiian ex-adman. It's one of the better ones with an interesting concentration on the Cook's many colourful characters. The Cook Islands, you soon realise after reading a few books on them, are a pretty small pool. The same big fish keep popping up in every account!

If you want to know more about what types of islands there are, how they are formed and what lives in the sea around them then *Exploring Tropical Isles & Seas* by Frederic Martini (Prentice-Hall, Englewood Cliffs, New Jersey, 1984) makes interesting reading.

If you just want a souvenir of the Cooks *Rarotonga* by James Siers (Millwood Press, Wellington, 1977) has some pretty though at times rather dated photos. If you're travelling further afield in the Pacific look for the excellent *South Pacific Handbook* by David Stanley (Moon Publications, Chico, California, 1986). Lonely Planet also has a growing list of individual guidebooks for Pacific nations – see the information page in the back of this book.

NEWSPAPERS & MEDIA

Rarotonga has a daily newspaper, the *Cook Islands News*. It provides a very brief summary of international events and a nearly equally brief coverage of local events. All in all it provides something between 30 and 60 seconds of reading time on an average day. Overseas papers and news magazines take a long time to get to the Cooks so you might as well get used to being out of touch with the outside world for the duration of your stay.

The Cooks have two local radio stations, one AM frequency and the other FM frequency, the first FM station in the south Pacific. Apart from local programmes they also broadcast Radio Australia's overseas news service. The advent of television is under discussion.

FILM & PHOTOGRAPHY

You can buy straightforward film – print film, Kodachrome 64, etc – at the duty free shops and other outlets in Rarotonga. Finding unusual film – Ektachrome, black & white film – is more difficult. And the prices, duty free or not, are very unexciting. Kodachrome 64 is approximately twice the price you pay at discount outlets in Australia. In other words bring your film with you!

The Cook Islanders are generally quite happy to be photographed but the usual rule applies – it's polite to ask first. It's also worth bringing some high speed film with you. If you're photographing in the densely forested mountain country of Rarotonga or in the *makatea* of Atiu it can be surprisingly dark. Bring a flash if you plan to visit the caves in Atiu or Mangaia.

HEALTH

The Cook Islands provide no unexpected

health risks apart from putting on weight through overeating and inactivity! At some times of year and in some places there are lots of mosquitoes but they're not malarial. Bring repellent. The water is drinkable and there are no risks from diseases of insanitation. No vaccinations are required unless you're arriving from an infected area. Of course, as at any tropical beach locale, you should beware of the sun. Don't overdo exposure on the first days and wear a good sun screen to protect against sunburn.

POST

Postage stamps are a major source of revenue for the government. They produce some beautiful stamps and by limiting the supply and availability they've managed to make many of them valuable collectors' items. The Cook Islands' Philatelic Bureau was set up by an American entrepreneur, Finbar Kenney. He was entangled in the late Sir Albert Henry's fly-in-the-voters programme in 1978 but despite NZ$80,000 in fines and court costs he continued to manage the lucrative stamp trade.

At the least, you can send some attractively stamped postcards home from the Cooks. Postage rates include:

	aerograms & postcards	air letters
Pacific	50c	55c
North America	55c	65c
Europe	60c	75c

TELEPHONE

On Rarotonga there is a modern phone system and a telephone office behind the post office. There are pay phones (but they refund your coin since local calls are free) in most hotels. On the outer islands, phone systems, if they exist at all, are not so modern. In Aitutaki, for example, all calls must still be placed through an operator.

ELECTRICITY

Electricity is 240 volts, 50 cycle AC just like in Australia and New Zealand and the same three-pin plugs are used. US two-pin plugs can often be bent to fit although, of course, the voltage is different. In Rarotonga the supply is regular and quite dependable. On smaller islands it may be available only when the generator is running and will shut down sometime in the evening. On very small islands plan on packing your own generator if you want power.

BUSINESS HOURS

Monday to Friday is the usual business week and shops are also open on Saturday mornings. They tend to open early (as early as 7 am for small trade stores) and close correspondingly early (3.30 to 4.30 pm is the usual shutting time). The main National Bank of New Zealand in Avarua, Rarotonga is open 9 am to 3 pm, Monday to Friday. The handful of other banks are usually open only 9 am to 12 noon. Nothing is open on Sunday – bars close at midnight on Saturday; even the two local airlines don't fly on Sundays.

TIME

The Cook Islands are east of the International Date Line. This is effectively one of the last places in the world; tomorrow starts later here than anywhere else. More precisely when it is 12 noon in the Cooks the time in other places (making no allowances for daylight saving and other seasonal variations) is:

Auckland, New Zealand	10 am next day
Sydney & Melbourne, Australia	8 am next day
San Francisco & Los Angeles, USA	3 pm
London, England	10 pm

Remember, however, that in common with many other places in the Pacific the Cook Islands also have Cook Islands Time, which means 'sometime, never, no hurry, no worries'.

The International Date Line

The early LMS missionaries generally came to the Cook Islands from Sydney, Australia and were unaware that they had crossed the International Date Line and should have turned the calendar back a day. This anomaly continued for 75 years until 1896 when Christmas was celebrated two days in a row and the Cooks came into line with the rest of the world. Or at least some of the Cooks came into line; it took a bit longer for the message to get to all the other islands and for it to be accepted. Accounts of visiting ships at that time indicate that considerable confusion existed for a while.

THEFT

Theft is not a problem in the Cook Islands and you have to be very slack to get anything stolen. People routinely leave car windows down (risking inundation from a sudden tropical downpour) and I've never seen so many cars and motorcycles standing around with their keys left in the ignition. I imagine a mugging would be a major event and so long as you don't leave cash heaped on your bedside table there doesn't seem to be too much theft from hotel rooms either.

Despite all this Maureen and I both had something stolen in the Cooks and both losses, we discovered afterwards, were fairly typical Cook Islands thefts. On the second night we were in the Cooks I lost a running shoe (that's right, just one) from the verandah in front of our room. I saw the thief: he was dark-brown, had floppy ears, a long tail, four legs and would have said 'woof' if I'd managed to catch him and ask him why the hell he took it. I never found it. Right at the end of the trip Maureen lost her bikini bottom (that's right, just the bottom) off the clothesline. Afterwards we were told that shoe-stealing dogs and off-the-clothesline knicker nickers were notorious. So watch out.

INFORMATION

If you want information on the Cook Islands you can write to the Cook Islands Tourist Authority, PO Box 14, Rarotonga, Cook Islands (tel 29-435, telex RG 62054). In New Zealand there's the Cook Islands Government Office in the Auckland suburb of Parnell or contact Travel Industry Services Ltd, PO Box 3647, Auckland (tel 79-4314). In Australia contact the Cook Islands Tourist Authority at Level 1, 92 Pitt St, Sydney, NSW 2000 (tel 232 7499) or the new Cook Islands airline, Cook Islands International, at 63 York St, Sydney, NSW 2000 (tel 268

1066). The Australian company Ansett Airlines manages and operates Cook Islands International so their offices can also provide information. Any Air New Zealand office should also be able to provide at least some information.

ACCOMMODATION

Although there is no visa requirement for most visitors to the Cooks there is one stipulation for all visitors – you must have pre-booked accommodation. This isn't quite as totalitarian as it sounds. For a start they don't say how long you have to book for – conceivably you could book for the first night only. Secondly there's nothing to stop you changing your mind as soon as you see the place you've booked into and to go looking elsewhere – some people do change their minds quite legitimately. And thirdly nobody really checks – you could easily walk out of the airport saying you'd booked into Hotel A or Z when you'd done nothing of the sort.

This rule is supposedly to stop people sleeping on beaches, camping out or staying with local people. The Cooks could indeed do with more cheap hostel accommodation or even a good campsite. At present camping is virtually impossible. People staying longer term often do rent houses locally. You can get quite a reasonable place for NZ$100 a week. No doubt some people stay with locals although it probably doesn't happen much on Rarotonga. On outer islands where accommodation is very limited you will have to stay with local people. On some islands – such as Mangaia – this is organised, arranged and prices are firmly set. On others, where visitors are few and far between, arrangements are likely to be very informal. In such a case make certain that you do not take advantage of Polynesian hospitality, be sure to pay your way.

Rarotonga is far and away the major attraction and it has far and away the most places to stay. There's a handful of places to stay on Aitutaki, a place or two at a few of the other islands but everything else is on Rarotonga. On Rarotonga there is one major hotel, some hostel-style accommodation and pretty much everything else is motel-style, closely related to the motels in New Zealand. This is no bad thing in one way – nearly every place has some sort of kitchen or cooking facilities and since restaurants tend to be limited, expensive, or scattered you may often find it more convenient and less expensive to fix your own food. It's also terrific if you have small children.

On the other hand it's a disappointment that the accommodation makes so little reference to the Pacific. The average Rarotongan motel could easily be in Newcastle, Australia or Palmerston North, New Zealand. They're dull, dull, dull. The *Atiu Motel* on Atiu, which makes extensive use of local materials, could show most places in Rarotonga how things can be done with just a little imagination.

FOOD & DRINK

Rarotonga has a surprising variety of surprisingly good restaurants. Elsewhere in the islands the choice of places to eat is likely to be much more limited. Even on Rarotonga the scattered locations of the places to stay and the places to eat mean you're quite likely to be either a long way from restaurants or find that the conveniently located eating places are very limited.

Fortunately most accommodation, particularly on Rarotonga, has kitchen facilities so you can fix your own food, and save some money along the way. The catch here is that much food is imported and is consequently expensive. There are a couple of ways of improving this situation. First of all look for local produce. There's little in the way of local packaged food apart from the expensive Frangi fruit juices and the terrible Vaiora soft drinks; virtually all other packaged food is imported (usually from New

Top: Cook Islands Christian Church, Titikaveka, Rarotonga (TW)
Left: Sunday Service at the CICC church, Arorangi, Rarotonga (TW)
Right: Gravestone, Titikaveka, Rarotonga (TW)

Top: Motorcycling the coast road, Atiu (TW)
Bottom: Typical island transport, Arorangi, Rarotonga (TW)

Zealand) and is very expensive. The price tags on anything from packaged cereal to yoghurt can be astonishing.

There are, however, plenty of locally grown fruits and vegetables. The trick is finding it – you're likely to do much better looking for it in local shops or even buying direct from the locals than from big supermarkets. Whereas locally grown vegetables can be very reasonably priced, in the supermarkets you often find the vegetables have come straight from New Zealand and cost several times the New Zealand or Australian prices. Bread is also baked locally on the larger islands and again is fairly reasonably priced.

The second way of economising is to bring some supplies with you. All food imports must be declared on arrival and although fresh produce may be confiscated you should have no problem with packaged goods. You can save some money by bringing your favourite breakfast cereal, rice, noodles, spaghetti, even packaged meals and the like.

Remember that just as costs on Rarotonga are much higher than in New Zealand, Australia or North America, costs are also much higher again on the outer islands than on Rarotonga. If you're going to the outer islands it's wise to bring some food supplies with you both for economy and variety. If you're going to a place with no formal accommodation it's only polite to supply as much food as you eat, and some more besides.

Local Food

You won't find too much local food on the restaurant menus but at 'Island Night' buffets or at barbecues you'll often find interesting local dishes. An *umakai* is a traditional feast cooked in an underground oven: food is *kai*, underground is *uma*.

Some dishes you might come across include:

breadfruit – spherical fruit which grows on trees to grapefruit size or larger.

They're so abundant they fall and squash on the roads everywhere. Breadfruit is more like a vegetable than a fruit and can be cooked in many ways, including like french fries.

eke – octopus

ika mata – marinated fish with coconut cream

kumara – sweet potato

poke – pawpaw pudding

puaka – suckling pig

taro – all purpose tuber vegetable. The roots are prepared rather like potato; the leaves, called *rukau*, can also be cooked and look and taste very much like spinach.

Drinks

The truly local drink is coconut water and for some reason Cook Islands coconuts are especially tasty. The most popular drink is beer – a wide variety of New Zealand beers are available plus Fosters (Australian), San Miguel (Philippines), Heineken (Dutch), Hinano (Tahitian), Viamo (Western Samoan). They cost around NZ$1.50 to 2.50 a can in bars and are cheaper from shops. Until independence Cook Islanders were strictly forbidden western alcohol which was, however, permitted to *papa'a*. Beer is a problem on the Cook Islands: far too much money gets spent on it and drunkenness is a social problem. Fortunately it's nowhere near as major a problem as it is in some countries in the region, Papua New Guinea in particular.

Although the beer is all imported there is a local soft drink bottling company called Vaiora – they make cola, lemonade, orange and other fairly awful imitations. Apart from the drinks being flat the bottles are notable for having labels that always fall off.

Try the excellent coffee from Atiu, and if you go to that island you should definitely try to go to a *tumunu* or bush beer-drinking session. *Tumunus* are also held on Mauke but although there is a bar named the Tumunu on Raro they are

really only found on those two islands. The old ritual *kava* ceremonies, to which the *tumunu* is related, were completely stamped out by the missionaries and are no longer found in any form.

Cannibalism

At one time the Cook Islanders certainly practised cannibalism. Although the early islanders rarely ate meat (their pigs were poor specimens and difficult to breed) there were plenty of fish and cannibalism was not, as it has been in some areas of the world, a protein supplement. It appears that in the Cooks it was an activity more closely associated with the supernatural acquisition of the *mana* or power of one's adversaries. To eat your defeated opponent was probably the most telling indignity you could subject him to. The pioneering missionary William Wyatt Gill reported the following cannibal recipe:

The long spear, inserted at the fundament, ran through the body, appearing again with the neck. As on a spit, the body was slowly singed over a fire, in order that the entire cuticle and all the hair might be removed. The intestines were next taken out, washed in sea-water, wrapped up in singed banana leaves (a singed banana-leaf, like oil-silk, retains liquid), cooked and eaten, this being the invariable perquisite of those who prepared the feast. The body was cooked, as pigs now are, in an oven specially set apart, red-hot basaltic stones, wrapped in leaves, being placed inside to insure its being equally done. The best joint was the thigh.

ART & CRAFTS

Although the arts and crafts of the Cook Islands today are only a shadow of their former importance they were once widespread and of high quality. The early missionaries, in their passion to obliterate all traces of heathenism, did a comprehensive job of destroying much of the old art forms but, fortunately, they also saved some of the best pieces, many of which can now be found in European museums.

There was no real connection between the southern high islands and the northern atolls in the pre-European period and the art of the small islands to the north is much more limited. Domestic equipment and tools, matting, and inlaid pearl shell on canoes and canoe paddles were about the extent of their work. In the south however, a variety of crafts developed with strong variations between the individual islands.

The Art of Tahiti by Terence Barrow (Thames & Hudson, London, 1979) is more accurately a guide to the art of Polynesia and includes an interesting chapter on the Cook Islands.

Wood Carving

Figures of gods carved from wood were amongst the most widespread art forms and were particularly common on Rarotonga. These squat figures, variously described as fisherman's gods or as images of specifically named gods such as Tangaroa, are similar to the Tangaroa image which has become symbolic of the Cook Islands today. Staff gods with repetitive figures carved down a pole, war clubs and spears were other typical Rarotongan artefacts. The incredibly

intricately carved mace gods, often from Mangaia, and the slab gods from Aitutaki, were other examples of wood carving which are no longer found today.

Ceremonial Adzes

Mangaian ceremonial adzes were an important craft now found only in museums. At first they probably had an everyday use but with time they became purely ceremonial objects and more and more stylised in their design. Each element of these adzes was beautifully made – from the stone blade to the carefully carved wooden handle and the intricate sennit binding that lashed the blade to the handle. Ceremonial adze making probably died out about 50 years ago.

Buildings

Houses and other buildings were made of natural materials which decayed rapidly so no ancient buildings survive to the present day and very few buildings of traditional construction remain on any of the southern islands. Wood carving was only rarely used in houses although some important buildings, including some of the first locally built mission churches, had carved and decorated wooden posts. Artistically impressive sennit lashing was, however, found on many buildings. Since nails were not available the wooden framework of a building was tied together with carefully bound sennit leaf. Each island or area had its own distinctive style for the plaiting of the sennit and this skill is still followed today. If you are on the island of Mangaia you can see fine sennit lashing on the roof beams of the CICC churches. Recently the Rarotongan Resort Hotel on Rarotonga has commissioned craftspeople to bind the beams of verandahs and walkways with sennit.

Other

Woven fans, feathered head-dresses bound with sennit, woven belts and baskets, and wooden seats from Atiu were other artistic crafts of the pre-European period. Some of these crafts have survived but most are found only in museums.

THINGS TO BUY

As important as what to buy in the Cooks is what not to buy. What not to buy is cheap tourist junk and there's lots of it. Tangaroa figures with spring-loaded, pop-up penises are about the most tasteless but there are plenty more where that came from. More insidious are the Cook Islands handicraft souvenirs that don't originate from the Cooks at all. A lot of the shell jewellery and wooden bowls were born in the Philippines! There are also plenty of New Zealand Maori items which the unscrupulous might try to pass off as Cook Islands Maori. In fact I'd be very suspicious of anything which could conceivably be made overseas – even supposedly indigenous items like Tangaroa figures. Fortunately the craft shops do seem to be remarkably honest and if you ask if a piece is local or made elsewhere you'll usually be given a straightforward answer.

Local arts and crafts include:

Tangaroa Figures

Tangaroa is the squat, ugly but well-endowed figure you find on the Cook Islands' one dollar coin. The God of Fertility he's become the symbol of the Cooks but it's been a long term rehabilitation because the early missionaries, in their zeal to wipe out all traces of heathenism, did a thorough job of destroying idols wherever they found them. Poor old Tangaroa, along with the rest of the old gods, was banned. When they did start to carve Tangaroa figures again they were often neuter, but now they're fully endowed once again. You can get Tangaroa figures ranging from key ring figures a couple of cm high up to huge ones standing a metre or more high and just about requiring a crane to move them. A figure about 25 cm high will cost around NZ$30.

Hats

The beautiful hats which all the women wear to church on Sundays are a Cook Islands speciality. These *rito* hats are woven of fine, bleached pandanus leaves and the best ones come from the islands of Rakahanga and Penrhyn. They cost from about NZ$50 so they're not cheap, but they're even more expensive in Tahiti.

Baskets

Some good quality basket work is still done but look out for plastic carton strapping and other man-made materials creeping into use.

Shell Jewellery

There's a lot of shell jewellery produced and also larger items like shell lamps. Some of this work is imported, principally from the Philippines, but some fine shell work is produced locally. Before you rush off to buy shells remember that something has to be evicted to provide the shell and conservationists are worried about some species being collected to extinction.

Tivaivai

These colourful and intricately sewn applique works are traditionally made as burial shrouds but are also used as bedspreads or simply as wall hangings. They're very rarely seen for sale.

WHAT TO BRING

The Cook Islands' balanced and moderate climate makes clothing choice a breeze – you rarely need anything warmer than a short-sleeve shirt or T-shirt but nor do you often find it too hot for comfort, the northern atolls apart. Remember, however, that these islands are relatively strait-laced and dress accordingly. Swimming gear is strictly for the beach and even on the beach going topless is frowned upon. Find an isolated beach before considering nudity – this is certainly not the Maldives if you're looking for an overall tan.

Bring an old pair of running shoes or sneakers for walking on the reefs. There are some things you'd rather not step on and coral cuts take a long time to heal. You'll also need those runners if you intend to go climbing or walking on Rarotonga or walking across the razor-sharp *makatea* on Atiu or Mangaia. Bring a torch (flashlight) if you're going to Atiu or Mangaia; it's essential equipment for exploring the caves. The Cook Islands are, of course, wonderful for snorkelling and you can either bring your own equipment with you or rent or buy it on Rarotonga.

The Cook Islands are a major supplier of clothes to New Zealand so there's a pretty good choice of clothes locally. Clothing apart, most western consumable commodities are readily available but prices are high. Better to bring a spare tube of toothpaste or another spool of film rather than have to buy it locally. Don't forget sun screen or suntan lotion although these are readily available.

The Cooks are a duty free port and there are a number of duty free shops in Avarua but the quantities they deal with are small so the prices, while a pretty good deal for Kiwis, will hardly be competitive with discount dealers in the USA, Europe or even Australia.

If you're planning to travel further afield, particularly if you travel deck class on the inter-island ships to the islands of the northern atolls, come prepared. You'll probably want a sleeping bag and some sort of foam mat to lay out on the deck. Cooking equipment and, of course, food supplies can also be useful.

Getting There

Occasionally a cruise ship might call on the Cooks, with great luck you might find a passenger-carrying freighter (the Rarotonga based Silk & Boyd ships occasionally sail to Samoa), and some yachts pass through (although the Cooks are nowhere near as popular for yachties as Tahiti, Fiji or Tonga). Basically, however, getting to the Cooks means flying and Rarotonga has the only international airport. Yachties can enter the Cooks at a couple of other islands.

Flying is easy from New Zealand or Australia, fairly easy from Tahiti, Samoa, Fiji and (believe it or not) Nauru, not so easy from elsewhere. At the moment there is no direct connection with the USA – visitors from North America have to come via Tahiti, Fiji or Samoa. Airlines who fly to the Cooks are Air New Zealand, Polynesian Airlines, Air Nauru and, most recently, Cook Islands International which is owned by the Cook Islands Government and operated by Ansett Airlines.

FROM NEW ZEALAND

Air New Zealand has three direct flights each week from Auckland and one weekly flight Auckland-Nadi (Fiji)-Rarotonga-Papeete (Tahiti) and the reverse. The regular one-way economy fare Auckland-Rarotonga is NZ$621 (double for return). Epic excursion return fares from Auckland range from NZ$812 in the low season to NZ$998 in the high season. To get the low fare you have to travel both directions in low seasons – if you travel one direction low and one direction high the fare is NZ$905. Cook Islands International also have one weekly flight Auckland-Rarotonga and the reverse. Fares are the same as for Air New Zealand.

FROM AUSTRALIA

Air New Zealand has connections from Australia with fares from Melbourne of A$872 in the low season, A$1046 in the high season. From Sydney the equivalent fares are A$793 and A$954. These are advance purchase fares which must be

booked 21 days in advance. There's an aircraft change in Auckland and you must either make careful plans to choose a good connection or spend some time in Auckland.

In late '86 Cook Islands International started a weekly direct flight from Sydney to Rarotonga and return. This brand new airline makes use of an Ansett Airlines Boeing 767 and is expected to increase the number of Australians visiting the islands. Fares are the same as with Air New Zealand and the flight takes about six hours. Group return fares ex-Sydney are A$750 and A$872 in the low and high season respectively and can be utilised by people visiting the islands on a package tour.

FROM NORTH AMERICA

There are no direct flights from the USA to the Cooks – you have to connect through Samoa or Tahiti. Advance purchase fares (14 days in advance) from the west coast to Auckland, New Zealand return, with a stopover in Rarotonga cost US$1046. Many more travellers are slotting in the Cooks on a trans-Pacific jaunt, often because of the attractive Circle Pacific tickets – see separate section, following.

FROM OTHER PACIFIC DESTINATIONS

Air New Zealand have a weekly Auckland-Nadi-Rarotonga-Papeete and reverse flight. Polynesian Airlines have a weekly flight Apia (Western Samoa)-Pago Pago (American Samoa)-Rarotonga-Papeete and the reverse and a second weekly flight which does not continue to Papeete. Air Nauru have a weekly flight Nauru-Pago Pago-Rarotonga-Niue-Auckland and the reverse.

CIRCLE PACIFIC FARES

Circle Pacific Fares are an extension of the popular Round The World tickets which allow you to combine the routes of two airlines and stop pretty much wherever you choose. Air New Zealand combines

with Cathay Pacific, Singapore Airlines or Thai International to offer a NZ$2711 (economy class) Circle Pacific Fare from New Zealand. From Australia the same ticket is A$1982 ex-Sydney or A$2032 ex-Melbourne.

From North America the official Circle Pacific fares are US$1870 or C$2394 and they can originate from Vancouver, San Francisco or Los Angeles. You can fly Air New Zealand through the South Pacific (including Rarotonga) to Australia and return with Thai International, Singapore Airlines, or Cathay Pacific through the North Pacific. Shop around as Circle Pacific fares are sometimes discounted several hundred dollars; they must be purchased 21 days in advance. For example, using one of these tickets you could fly Los Angeles-Honolulu-Papeete-Rarotonga-Nadi-Auckland-Sydney-Los Angeles. Usually four stop-overs are included free but there is an extra cost for additional stop-overs.

Air New Zealand also combine with Polynesian Airlines for a Circle Epic fare which allows you to loop out from Auckland to Tonga, Apia, Rarotonga and back to Auckland for NZ$1180. Or you can get a Polynesian Polypass for US$799 (A$1165) which is valid for 30 days and allows you to fly anywhere on the Polynesian Airlines route network during that period. Polynesian fly from Sydney and Auckland to numerous Pacific Islands including Rarotonga, Western and American Samoa, Tahiti, Niue, Tonga and Fiji.

DEPARTURE TAX
There's a NZ$20 departure tax when you fly out of Rarotonga; for children aged two to 12 it's NZ$10.

Flying to the Cooks
Aviation in the Cook Islands has had quite an interesting history. During WW II, airstrips were built on Penrhyn, Aitutaki and Rarotonga and in 1945 a DC3 service operated every two weeks on a Fiji-Tonga-Western Samoa-Aitutaki-Rarotonga route. This service by New Zealand National Airways Corporation was dropped in 1952 but Tasman Empire Airways Limited had meanwhile started a monthly Solent flying boat service on the 'Coral Route' from Auckland to Papeete via Fiji and Aitutaki. See the Aitutaki section for more details on this route.

The Solent service was increased to once every two weeks and continued until 1960. For a time there were no flights at all to the Cooks apart from infrequent New Zealand Air Force flights. In 1963 Polynesian Airways started a service from Apia in Western Samoa to Rarotonga but this was stopped in 1966 due to new regulations banning small aircraft making such long-distance flights over water. Once again the Cook Islands were left without international connections and it was not until the new airport was opened in the early '70s and big jets could fly into Rarotonga that flights resumed.

YACHTIES
The Cook Islands are not a major Pacific yachting destination like French Polynesia, Tonga or Fiji. Nevertheless a steady trickle of yachts do pass through the islands. Official entry points are Penrhyn in the northern group and Aitutaki and Rarotonga in the southern group. Many yachties only visit the uninhabited atoll of Suwarrow in the northern group – illegally if they haven't already officially entered the country. Yachties are liable for the departure tax just like people who arrive by air.

Getting Around

There are basically just three ways of getting from island to island around the Cooks (if you don't own your own yacht). In the southern group you can fly with Air Rarotonga or Cook Islandair or you can take the inter-island freight ships of Silk & Boyd Lines. If you want to go to the northern islands you've got no choice – uncomfortable freighters are all there is on offer! There are airstrips on a couple of the northern islands but the distances are so great that the cost of flying to them in the small aircraft used around the southern islands would be prohibitive.

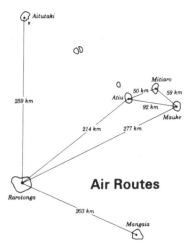

Air Routes

AIR

Cook Islandair (CI) has Air New Zealand as its majority owner and operates a single, nine-seater Britten-Norman Islander aircraft. Air Rarotonga (AR) is privately owned and operates a couple of Beechcraft. Between them they fly to Aitutaki (both airlines), Atiu (both), Mauke (CI), Mitiaro (CI) and Mangaia (AR). One-way fares (double for return) include Rarotonga-Aitutaki NZ$74 (CI) or NZ$95 (AR); Rarotonga-Mauke NZ$74 (CI); Rarotonga-Atiu NZ$66 (CI) NZ$85 (AR); Rarotonga-Mangaia NZ$85 (AR); Mauke-Atiu NZ$45 (CI). Children fly at half fare. The chart illustrates the possible routes.

There's quite a contrast between the two airlines: Air Rarotonga is much more 'with it' than Cook Islandair. Cook Islandair's schedules seem to be some sort of pipe dream; when you actually try to pin them down on when flights might leave nothing is simple. Air Rarotonga is also somewhat more expensive.

Both airlines have special fare deals. If you pay a week ahead Cook Islandair offers fare reductions, for example Rarotonga-Aitutaki-Rarotonga costs NZ$119 instead of NZ$148. Air Rarotonga offers through fares so that if, for example, you're flying Rarotonga-Atiu-Rarotonga-Mangaia-Rarotonga you can get a special Atiu-Mangaia through fare which reduces the total cost from NZ$340 to NZ$281. You have to fly on the next available flight but it doesn't matter if that 'connecting' flight is several days later.

Nobody flies anywhere on Sunday. The rest of the week Air Rarotonga flies to

Aitutaki two or three times daily. They also fly to Atiu three times a week and to Mangaia twice a week. Cook Islandair flies to Aitutaki twice daily. They fly to Atiu and Mauke about two or three times a week, and Mitiaro about once a week, depending on which way the connections go. In 1986 Air Rarotonga were buying an old, four-engine De Havilland Heron. This aircraft will give them greater passenger capacity and could also allow them to fly to islands in the northern group if demand was there.

The airlines addresses are:

Air Rarotonga
  PO Box 79, Rarotonga, Cook Islands (tel 22-888, telex 62036)
Cook Islandair
  PO Box 65, Rarotonga, Cook Islands (tel 23-304, telex AIR NZ 2541, attn Cook Islandair)

Flying in the Cooks

If you haven't flown on small local carriers like Air Raro' and Cook Islandair you've got quite a treat in store. For a start they don't just weigh your baggage, they weigh you as well. Secondly they usually have to arrange the passengers for the best weight distribution – on Air Raro's Beechcraft this means putting the heavies up front. I made one flight where two super-heavies at the front had real difficulty getting their belts round their middles. I usually seemed to be right at the back!

It's out on the outer islands, however, that you get the real feel for island flying. At the airstrips all and sundry turn out to see the planes come and go and to welcome and farewell travellers. Usually they simply drive their trucks out and park them around the aircraft to load and unload. Departures are tearful occasions and the passengers usually leave loaded down with colourful and fragrant *eis*. In fact some flights depart looking like aerial florist's shops and the perfume inside can be quite overpowering!

SHIP

Shipping services have had a colourful history in the Cooks: companies have come and gone, ships have run onto reefs,

fortunes have been made but more often lost. Despite the increasing use of air services shipping is still of vital importance to the islands. The northern islands can only be served by ship and throughout the islands ships are necessary to bring in commodities and export produce.

Shipping in the islands has two major problems to face. First of all there are simply too few people and they're too widely scattered to be easily and economically serviced. From the ship owners' point of view shipping between the islands is only feasible with a government subsidy. From the islanders' point of view it's difficult to produce export crops if you can't be certain a ship will be coming by at the appropriate time to collect them.

The second problem is that the islands generally have terrible harbours. The south sea image of drifting through a wide passage in the reef into the clear sheltered waters of the lagoon doesn't seem to apply to the Cooks. In the northern atolls the reef passages are generally too narrow or shallow to allow large ships to enter. In the southern volcanic islands the passages through the fringing reefs are usually too small to let a ship enter and dock. Even Rarotonga's main harbour Avatiu is too small for large ships – or even too many small ones. All this means that ships have to anchor outside the reef and transfer passengers and freight to shore by lighters. At some of the islands even getting the lighters through the narrow reef passages is a considerable feat. Unless conditions are ideal it's not even possible to anchor offshore at some of the Cook Islands and freighters have to be under way constantly, even while loading and unloading.

The Cook Islands' shipping service is operated by the two-ship company of Silk & Boyd. Don Silk and Bob Boyd turned up in Rarotonga on their way across the Pacific from New Zealand on their yacht. Their Pacific cruise ended right there when they bought a recently wrecked ketch and found themselves in the shipping business. Today their two Scandinavian-built ships, the 50 metre (164 foot), 400 ton *Manuvai* and *Mataora* carry freight and passengers throughout the islands and to neighbouring Samoa.

If you plan to explore the outer islands by ship you need to be flexible and hardy. Schedules are hard to pinpoint and unlikely to be kept to. You have to visit the Silk & Boyd office beside the Avatiu harbour in Avarua and find out where the ships are and where they're going. Office hours are Monday to Friday from 8 am to 4 pm. Along the way schedules are quite likely to change – weather, breakdowns, loading difficulties or unexpected demands can all put a kink in the schedule.

On board the ships, conditions are cramped and primitive: these are not luxury cruise ships. They're also small and the seas in this region are often rough. If you're at all prone to seasickness you'll definitely spend time hanging your head over the side. There are two classes of accommodation on board: cabin class and deck class. Cabin class means you get a cabin – or at least a bunk in a cabin. In deck class you're out on the open deck with everybody else. If it's hot and still it's much more comfortable on deck. If it's pouring with rain you'll wish you were in a cabin. Food in cabin class is usually pretty reasonable, so long as you're not seasick. In deck class you provide your own food.

Fortunately the trips are usually not too long and many of the islands are only a day's travel apart. Few are more than two or three days apart. In the southern group, fares for a single hop start at NZ$30.80 for deck class, NZ$60 for cabin class and go up to NZ$85 and NZ$220 respectively if you have to go to five or six islands before reaching your destination. A Rarotonga out-to-one-island and return trip costs NZ$60 and NZ$100 respectively.

Fares are not so simple in the northern group – it depends on where you go and what route you take. Some sample fares include:

	deck	cabin
Rarotonga-Rakahanga	NZ$ 83.25	NZ$249.00
Rarotonga-Palmerston	NZ$ 33.65	NZ$ 92.40
Aitutaki-Penrhyn	NZ$ 74.25	NZ$173.70
Aitutaki-Manihiki	NZ$ 62.95	NZ$210.00
Rarotonga-Pukapuka	NZ$ 88.20	NZ$294.50
complete Northern Group	NZ$255.00	NZ$780.00

Only cabin class fares are available to the less frequently covered international destinations. Rarotonga to Niue is NZ$200, to Pago Pago (American Samoa) NZ$250, to Apia (Western Samoa) NZ$275.

The Silk & Boyd office address is PO Box 131, Rarotonga, Cook Islands – telex RG 62042 Traders, cable SilkBoyd or tel 22-442.

Why They Don't Run to Schedule

In Aitutaki we met a group of marine geologists from Fiji, a woman off to Manihiki to research musical instruments and other associated artefacts, and a man off on a loop around the northern islands. Supposedly two days out from Rarotonga towards Manihiki, the ship was already four days behind schedule.

Day one was lost at Mauke when it was too rough and they had to wait for conditions to improve before unloading. Day two was lost because although the ship was not supposed to be going to Aitutaki in the first place it had been diverted there because of the marine geologists and all their equipment. Then

because of the day lost at Mauke the ship arrived at Aitutaki on a Sunday instead of a Saturday. Since no work gets done on a Sunday they couldn't unload and another day was lost. On Sunday night a ferocious wind blew up (some yachties told us the next morning they recorded wind speeds of 50 knots) and continued all day Monday – so again there was no unloading. The marine geologists spent the day climbing hills to see if they could spot the ship, with their equipment, offshore. It had moved round to the other side of the island to shelter from the wind.

On Tuesday we flew back to Rarotonga, leaving them all wondering whether they would get their gear off that day and if the ship would be continuing north that night.

LOCAL TRANSPORT

On Rarotonga there's a bus service, lots of taxis, lots of rental cars, and rental motorcycles and pushbikes. On Aitutaki there are a handful of taxis, lots of rental motorcycles and bicycles. On Atiu the sole place to stay has a number of motorcycles to rent. Elsewhere you can walk.

The Southern Group

Rarotonga and Aitutaki are the most important southern islands and 99% of visitors to the Cook Islands get no further than these two islands. A trickle do continue to the other islands of the southern group, fewer still to the northern group.

The southern group of islands are larger in terms of both size and population than the northern islands. These volcanic islands are also economically better off than the coral atolls of the northern group.

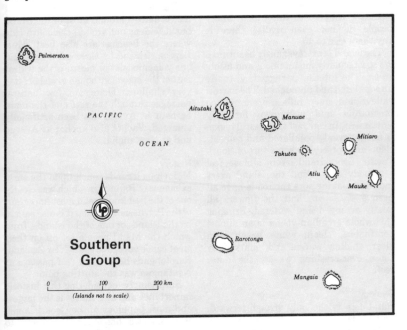

Rarotonga

Population: 9530
Area: 67.2 square km

Rarotonga is not only the major island and population centre of the Cook Islands it's also, like Tahiti in French Polynesia, virtually synonymous with the whole island chain. Nobody goes to the Cook Islands – they go to Rarotonga. Many people do not even realise there is anywhere else to go.

The island is extravagantly beautiful – it's spectacularly mountainous and lushly green. The interior is rugged, virtually unpopulated and untouched. The narrow valleys and steep hills are simply too precipitous and overgrown for easy settlement. In contrast the coastal region is fertile, evenly populated and as neat, clean and 'pretty' as some sort of South Pacific Switzerland. You almost feel somebody zips round the island every morning making sure the roads have all been swept clean and the flowers all neatly arranged and watered. Fringing this whole arcadian vision is an almost continuous, clean, white beach with clear, shallow waters and, marked by those ever-crashing waves, the outer reef.

Geology

Rarotonga is the only straightforward, high volcanic island on the Tahiti model in the Cook Islands. The inland area is mountainous with steep valleys, razorback ridges and swift-flowing streams. Most of this area is covered with dense jungle. Rarotonga is the youngest of the Cook Islands: the volcanic activity which thrust it above sea level occurred more recently than on any of the other islands. The major mountains of the island are the remains of the outer rim of the cone. The cone is open on the north side and Maungatea rises in the very centre.

The narrow coastal plain with its swampy area close to the hills is somewhat akin to the raised, outer coral fringe or *makatea* of several other islands in the southern group. On Rarotonga the plains are far more fertile than on islands like Mitiaro, Atiu, Mangaia or Mauke.

The lagoon within Rarotonga's outer reef is narrow around most of the island but it widens out around the south side where the beaches are also best. Muri Lagoon, fringed by three sand cays and one volcanic islet or *motu*, is the widest part of the lagoon although even here it is very shallow. There are few natural passages through the reef and the main harbour at Avatiu has been artificially enlarged. Yachts also anchor at Avarua and at Ngatangiia.

History

Numerous legends touch upon the early existence of Rarotonga which was clearly one of the best known and most important of the Polynesian islands. It is also said to be the island, or one of the islands, from which the Maori people set off on their great canoe voyage to settle New Zealand. Rarotongans believe the reef passage at Ngatangiia was the starting point.

Surprisingly, considering this historic importance and also that it is the largest and most populous of the Cook Islands, Rarotonga was one of the later islands to be 'discovered' by Europeans. The first discovery can probably be credited to the mutineers on the *Bounty*, who happened upon Rarotonga after they had returned to Tahiti and were searching for a remote island where they could hide from the British Navy. This was probably some time in late 1789, but, and this is hardly surprising, the mutineers didn't have much to say about their important discovery.

In any case the mutineers did not set

Traditional Wedding March

foot upon Rarotonga; nor did the crew of Captain Cook's *Endeavour* who sighted the island in 1813. Their suggestion that the island might have sandalwood – a valuable commodity – led to the next visitor. Philip Goodenough, captain of the *Cumberland*, showed up in 1814 and spent three months on Rarotonga; three less than harmonious and peaceful months. Unable to find any sandalwood the crew of the *Cumberland* decided to take back *nono* wood instead. This was an unsuccessful gamble as *nono* wood turned out to be of negligible value.

During their stay at Ngatangiia the crew managed to get themselves involved in a number of local squabbles which resulted in the deaths of a number of the crew, including Goodenough's female companion, and, of course, numerous Rarotongans. Eventually the *Cumberland* left Rarotonga in some haste, but two local women and a man were taken with them and left at their next stop, Aitutaki. William Gill later described the *Cumberland's* visit to Rarotonga as a 'continued series of rapine, cruelty, vice and bloodshed.' Understandably, Goodenough

did not go into great detail about his adventures so Rarotonga remained comparatively unknown. In the following years a number of vessels visited Rarotonga but none stayed for more than short periods.

In 1821 Papeiha, the Polynesian missionary or 'teacher' from Raiatea in the Society Islands, was landed in Aitutaki and in 1823 the English missionary John Williams went to Aitutaki to see how successful he had been. Papeiha had done remarkably well so Williams and Papeiha set off to convert Rarotonga, leaving two other Polynesian missionaries on Aitutaki to carry on the work. They took with them the Rarotongan women whom Goodenough had left on Aitutaki nine years earlier, together with two Rarotongan men who had somehow found their way to Aitutaki by canoe.

Despite the fact that they had Rarotongan passengers on board, the island proved elusive and after a week's futile search they gave up and made for the island of Mangaia instead. The Mangaians, who to this day have a reputation for being a dour and unfriendly lot, certainly did not rush out to greet the arrival of Christianity with open arms and the missionaries soon sailed on. Their next stop was Atiu, the main island of the group known as Nga-pu-toru which also includes Mauke and Mitiaro. Here Williams convinced Rongomatane, a notorious cannibal king, to embrace Christianity. This was achieved in a remarkably short time and the neighbouring islands of Mauke and Mitiaro were converted with equally amazing rapidity due to Rongomatane's assistance. As a finale Rongomatane, who had never been to Rarotonga, gave Williams sailing directions which were spot on.

As he had been on Aitutaki, Papeiha was left on the island to convince the islanders to give up their earlier religion and take on the new one. And, as on Aitutaki, he succeeded with thoroughness and surprising speed. Four months later additional Polynesian missionaries were landed to assist Papeiha and in little more than a year after his arrival Christianity had taken firm hold. The first permanent *papa'a* missionaries were Charles Pitman and John Williams who came to Rarotonga in 1827, followed a year later by Aaron Buzacott. Between them these three men translated the entire Bible into Maori and Buzacott also established the village of Arorangi which was to be a model for new villages on the island. The missionaries wished to gather the previously scattered population together in order to speed the propagation of Christianity.

Cannibalism may have been stamped out but the arrival of Christianity was not all peace and light. The indigenous culture was destroyed and missionaries also brought epidemics of previously unknown diseases: dysentery, whooping cough, mumps and measles were just some of them. From an estimated 6000 to 7000 people on Rarotonga when Christianity arrived the population had fallen to 2800 in 1848 and in another 20 years to less than 2000.

Although the missionaries tried to exclude other Europeans from settling more and more whalers and traders visited the island. In 1850-51 more than 20 trading ships and 60 whalers paused at Rarotonga and Buzacott's wife lamented that men of 'some wealth and little religious principle' were settling on the island. The Rarotongans had been firmly warned to beware of the French, however, who had taken over Tahiti in 1843. The dangers of Papism were a major worry for the London Missionary Society!

In 1865 the Rarotongan *ariki*, frightened by rumours of French expansionary intent, requested British protection for the first time. This request was turned down but in the following years the missionaries' once absolute power declined as more Europeans came to the island and trade grew. Finally in 1888 a British protectorate was formally declared over the southern islands and Rarotonga became the unofficial capital of the group.

What to do with the islands next was a subject of some controversy but eventually in 1901 they were annexed to newly independent New Zealand and the close relationship between the two countries that continues to this day was established.

Orientation

Finding your way around Rarotonga is admirably easy – there's a coastal road around the edge and a lot of mountains in the middle. Basically it's that simple. A number of roads run inland from the coast but if you want to get all the way into the middle, or cross the island from one side to the other, you have to do it on foot.

AVARUA

Avarua, the capital of the Cook Islands and the main town, lies in the middle of the north coast stretch, a couple of km to the east of the airport. It's a sleepy, little port, very much the image of a south seas trading centre. Nearly everything it has to offer can be found along the waterfront

Top: Muri Lagoon *motus* (islets) and the south-east coast of Rarotonga (TW)
Bottom: Sunset at Arorangi, Rarotonga (TW)

Top: South coast scene, Rarotonga (TW)
Left: The Needle, (Te Rua Manga), cross-island trek, Rarotonga (TW)
Right: Cricket in the tropics, Rarotonga (TW)

Tepou, A Rarotongan Chief

road. Avarua doesn't demand a lot of your time but it does have a small, interesting museum, a fine old church, a couple of interesting shipwrecks and one of the best bars in the Pacific.

Information

Tourist Office The Cook Islands Tourist Authority has an office right in the middle of Avarua. They have the usual sort of tourist office information including copies of *What's On in the Cook Islands*, an excellent annually produced adverts-and-information guide to Rarotonga and Aitutaki. There's also a good bulletin board with info on inter-island shipping services and flights. The office is open Monday to Friday from 8 am to 4 pm, Saturday from 9 am to 12 noon.

Post Office The Central Post Office is just off the main road in Avarua. It's open 8 am to 4 pm on weekdays, not at all on weekends. Poste Restante is handled at the very first counter; they usually seem to have only a dozen or so letters waiting for visitors. With the relative infrequency of flights to the Cook Islands it depends when letters are mailed how long they take but even to or from Europe letters seem to make it in a week.

The Cook Islands' stamps are collector's items – lots of letters go out with far more stamps on them than are strictly necessary. Right across the road from the Post Office there's a philatelic department if you want mint copies; they also have sets of Cook Islands coins. There are no Cook Islands notes but there is a coin equivalent to each New Zealand coin plus the weighty Cook Islands dollar coin.

Banks In Avarua the National Bank of New Zealand is open 9 am to 3 pm on weekdays. If you haven't been able to find a Cook Islands dollar as a souvenir they also have them. Travellers' cheques and major currencies in cash can also be changed at larger stores and hotels.

Books & Maps The Bounty Bookshop at Cook's Corner has a reasonably good selection of books and magazines. They also have a small selection of books on the Cook Islands and other Pacific destinations. You'll find interesting titles you may not even have heard of elsewhere although the choice is small. Several other places also have books on the Cooks and other places in the South Pacific. Try Island Crafts, the Cook Islands Trading Company and in particular the Rarotonga Library; between them you'll find a surprising variety of titles. Right across the road from the Library and Museum the University of the South Pacific Centre sells books published by USP.

The Survey Department office behind the Central Post Office has maps of the Cook Islands. There are excellent maps of Rarotonga and Aitutaki and they may have maps of equally good quality for some other islands. If not they can

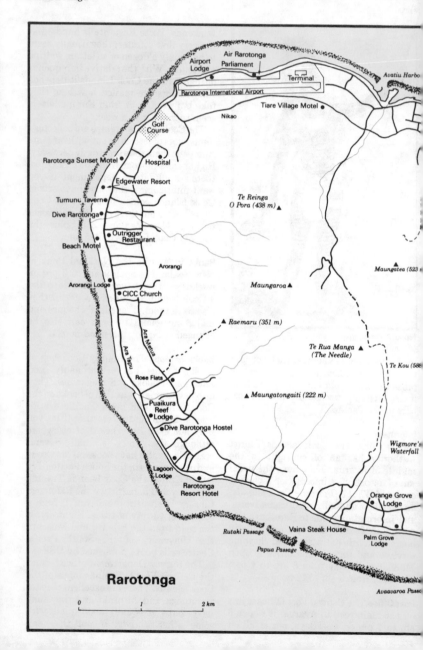

Rarotonga

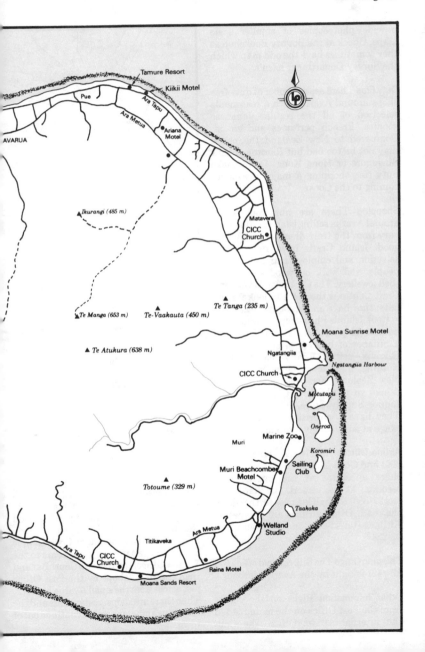

provide photocopies of smaller scale maps. Check at the Bounty Bookshop as they sometimes have the odd map which the Survey Department hasn't.

Duty Free There are a number of duty free shops around Avarua with a reasonable selection of all the regular Japanese goodies, French perfumes and so on. Compared to New Zealand the prices may not be too bad but Rarotonga isn't Singapore or Hong Kong. Don't make duty free shopping a major reason for coming to the Cooks.

Shopping There are numerous shops around Avarua selling island crafts – they vary from the truly dreadful to the very good. Island Crafts have an excellent selection and employ their own craftspeople who work on woodcarving and shell jewellery. The Cook Islands Women's Craft Centre is the place to look for rito hats; they have an excellent selection.

Cook Islands Photographics offers four hour developing of colour film. There are a number of boutiques, such as Joyce Peyroux, selling locally manufactured clothing, most of which is exported to New Zealand. For beer, wine or other drinks go to the government operated Liquor Supply Store, near the airport. They have a surprisingly international range at surprisingly reasonable prices.

Airline Offices Air New Zealand (tel 26-300) and Cook Islandair (also tel 26-300) share an office at the international terminal at the airport. Air Rarotonga (tel 22-888) is a half km or so further down the road. Other airlines are Polynesian Airlines (tel 23-669) and Air Nauru (tel 22-224).

Shipping Office The Silk & Boyd office (tel 22-442) is right by the Avatiu Harbour.

Other Information Right on the corner from the Post Office on the main road in the Internal Affairs Office, the Con-

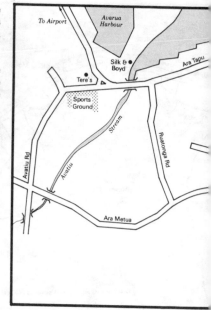

servation Officer has a good leaflet (50c) on walking routes around the island. See the section on walking in this chapter.

Orientation
Finding your way around Avarua is no problem – there's really only one road and that is right along the waterfront. Starting from the western (airport) end of town some local landmarks include the main harbour of Avatiu, then the shops, Bank, petrol station and so on along the inland side of the road. There's a grassy strip along the coast side where you also find the bus shelter and the small open market. Beyond the major Cook Islands Trading Company shop you come to the Tourist Office, the Banana Court Bar and then the roundabout by the Post Office just across from the small Avarua harbour. Then there are shops, restaurants and the town's two cinemas as you continue out of town.

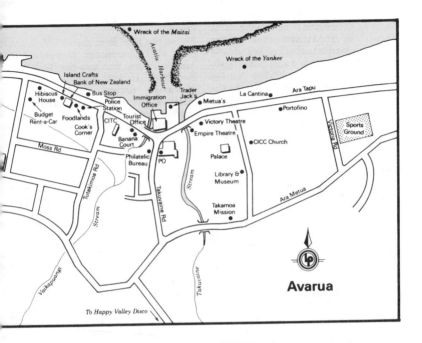

Avarua

Wreck of the Maitai

Directly offshore from the centre of Avarua is the wreck of the *SS Maitai*, a 3393 ton Union Steam Ship vessel which used to trade between the Cook Islands and Tahiti. She ran on to the reef, fortunately without loss of life, on 24 December 1916. Her cargo included a number of Model T Fords. All that remains today is her boiler, just off the edge of the fringing reef. In the '50s a couple of enterprising New Zealanders brought up one of ship's bronze propellers.

Wreck of the Yankee

On 24 July 1964 the brig *Yankee* broke her mooring line in a gale and ran onto the reef at the western end of Avarua. All that remains today is her rusting hull, high and dry on the reef. You can easily walk out to her. This much photographed hulk was equally well recorded during her heyday as she was once operated by the

National Geographic magazine and appeared in numerous magazine articles in the 1950s.

The *Yankee* had a long and interesting history before her ignominious end. The 30 metre (97 foot), 117 ton, steel-hulled vessel was originally built in 1912 in Germany but was taken by the British as a war prize after WW I. She served as the North Sea pilot vessel *Duhnen* until she was bought by Irving and Electra Johnson in 1946. Overhauled and re-rigged as a brigantine in Devonshire she carried 723 square metres (7775 square feet) of sail when fully rigged and circled the world no less than seven times before finally being sold to Miami-based Windjammer Cruises in 1957. Earlier that year she had visited the Cooks with the Johnsons and she returned with her new owners in 1961.

On her third visit in 1964 she was in sorry condition and, say the pundits, her crew was too busy partying on with

Rarotongan bar-girls to handle the storm when it blew up. At that time there was no regular air service to the Cook Islands and it took a long time to ship her irate American passengers out. You can see some mementos from the *Yankee* in the museum, just up the road from her rusting remains. Over the years storms have pushed her further and further up the reef until now the remains are nearly at the beach.

Church

The CICC church in Avarua is a fine, old, white painted building from very much the same mould as other CICC churches in the Cooks. It was built in 1853 when Aaron Buzacott was the resident missionary. The interesting graveyard around the church is worth a leisurely browse. At the front you'll find a monument to the pioneering Polynesian 'teacher' Papeiha. Just to the left (as you face the church) is the grave of Albert Henry, the first prime minister of the independent Cook Islands. Other well-known people buried here include author Robert Dean Frisbie.

Palace

Across the road from the church is the ruins of Taputapuatea, the palace of Makea Takau, who was the 'Queen of Rarotonga' in 1888 when the London Missionary Society withdrew to the sidelines and the British government officially took control of the Cook Islands (or at least the southern group) and forestalled any possibility of a French takeover from Tahiti.

Library & Museum

The small Library with its friendly staff has a collection of Pacific literature locked away which, if you enquire, you may be able to inspect and read – but only on the premises. The little Museum has an interesting collection of ancient tools, carved figures, and other historical items, even a beautiful outrigger canoe. There's no admission charge but a donation is appreciated. The opening hours are Monday to Friday 9 am to 4.30 pm, Tuesday and Thursday evenings 7 to 8.30 pm, Saturday mornings 9 am to 12 noon.

Just down beyond the Library and

Avarua Church

Museum is the Takamoa Mission House of 1842. One of the earliest mission buildings on the island it is still in original condition.

Tours

There are a variety of tour operators on Rarotonga. Probably the best known is Exham Wichman who operates daily tours from Arorangi. His 'Life Style Tour' takes you along the inland roads to see crops and plantations and explains the land ownership system. It continues with a visit to the CICC church and concludes with a refreshment stop at Exham's home. This tour costs NZ$15. Other tours include a Historical Tour (NZ$12 or 18 with lunch), Flowers Tour (NZ$12) and a Cemetery Tour (NZ$12). If you book directly with Exham (tel 21-180) you get a 10% discount.

Three other companies – Union Citco, Tipani Tours and Trans Pacific Travel – also operate a variety of tours. Typical tours include a round-the-island tour or if you're feeling energetic an across-the-island trek. There are historic tours, cultural tours, visits to the beaches and the Muri Lagoon motus, garden tours, agricultural tours and various other specialist tours. For the drinkers Union Citco even have a pub crawl with 10 half-hour stops at notable island watering holes. They also have an exclusive tour to the Albert Henry Museum with its collection of memorabilia of the late prime minister, a historic tour and a garden tour. Tipani also have day-trips to Aitutaki, as do Air Rarotonga. Trans Pacific Travel also have tours.

Dive Rarotonga operate diving trips every day and also have an air-filling station and diving gear for sale or hire. The trips last about three hours and with one tank of air cost NZ$35 or NZ$30 if you have your own gear. Dive Rarotonga is on the airport side of Arorangi (near the Edgewater Resort) and a popular diving spot is just outside the reef off Arorangi.

Air Rarotonga operate flightseeing tours of Rarotonga – if two people turn up, each with NZ$32 in hand, they'll send you up right away if the plane and the pilot are handy. You get about 20 minutes of Raro from above and a good chance to work out exactly where those mountain trails go and where the good diving spots are.

Places to Stay

Normally in our guidebooks we categorise accommodation by price and then, if necessary, sub-categorise it by location. This policy doesn't work so well with Rarotonga where the places to stay are simply dotted round the coast road. There's no 'cheap enclave' or 'top end ghetto'. In fact there's really not much at the top and bottom ends at all. Nearly everything is somewhere in the middle! The list that follows simply works its way round the island in a counterclockwise direction from the airport. Each hotel is followed by its km distance from the centre of town, first in a counterclockwise then a clockwise direction, and then its price category – bottom, top and middle. The airport terminal is 2.5 km from the town centre, counterclockwise; the total distance around the island is 32.5 km.

Almost every place to stay shares one basic similarity with its competitors: they nearly all offer some sort of kitchen or cooking facilities. This is great if you have kids or are trying to economise since you can prepare your own food at some financial saving over eating out. Since accommodation and restaurants both tend to be scattered it's also a considerable convenience – if you don't feel like eating out in the same place every meal of your stay.

Rarotongan Sunset Motel (tel 28-028, telex RG 62074), (6 km, 26.5 km, middle). The first place you come to when moving round the island counterclockwise is the brand new Sunset Motel which only opened in mid-86. It has 20 self-contained units with the usual motel-style mod cons including well-equipped kitchen facilities. There's a guest laundry, freshwater pool and a video unit in every room with daily in-house videos. Twelve of the rooms can be interconnected. Prices are NZ$55 (single or double) or NZ$65 for the nine beachfront units. Extra people cost NZ$10 each but children under two are free.

Edgewater Motel (tel 25-437, telex RG62016), (7 km, 25.5 km, middle). A major expansion programme in 1986 took the Edgewater to 178 rooms making it the biggest resort in the Cook Islands. It's a combination between a resort hotel and the motel-style accommodation found at most places on Rarotonga. There's a bar, restaurant and various entertainment facilities but there are also cooking facilities in all the rooms. The rooms are quite straightforward with the three different categories differing mainly in their furnishings. Singles/doubles start at NZ$55/58, go up to NZ$60/64 and NZ$65/ 69. Extra people cost NZ$4 in the cheapest rooms, NZ$5 in the other categories.

There's a saltwater swimming pool and the resort is right on the beach although it's not one of the best stretches of beach.

Beach Motel (tel 27-340, telex RG 62060) (8 km, 24.5 km, middle). Next up is the 20-room Beach Motel, another uninspired but comfortable and well-kept place. The rooms all have useful little kitchens and it's right on the beach. The water is very shallow and the coral is not very good but it's OK for splashing around and lackadaisical snorkelling. The beach is just fine and also offers excellent sunsets. The *Beach Bar* is popular, not only with guests but also with outsiders. Fortunately for the residents it never seems to get too noisy for comfort, except on Sunday evenings when the barbecue and island dance performance, a major Rarotongan event, is held. After all, anywhere else on

Sunday, church services are about all there is going on. Double rooms are NZ$59 or NZ$69 for the beachfront units plus NZ$10 for each extra person.

Are-Renga Motel (tel 20-050), (8.5 km, 23 km, bottom end). There are eight units in this very straightforward motel on the inland side of the road through Arorangi. Rooms cost just NZ$20/25/30 for singles/ doubles/triples and although they're not the latest thing they all have attached bathrooms and kitchen facilities. If you're looking for something low priced you may well find them ideal.

Arorangi Lodge (tel 27-379), (8.5 km, 23 km, bottom end). On the coast side of the road just a little further into Arorangi there are eight well-equipped and well-kept units. Costs are NZ$35/45 for singles/doubles plus NZ$6 for each extra person. They'll put as many beds in a room as you want and they also quote lower off-season rates so this is another place worth considering if you're economising.

Whitesands Motel (tel 25-789) (11 km, 21.5 km, bottom end). On the beach side of the road at the far end of Arorangi there are six units with kitchen facilities, facing right on to the beach. Prices are NZ$30/ 36/48 for singles/doubles/triples but unfortunately they're not very well kept or well equipped; you'll do better elsewhere.

Rose Flats (11 km, 21.5 km, bottom end), (tel 27-777). On the Ara Metua, about 400 metres off the coast road at the southern end of Arorangi, these flats are very straightforward but also low priced at NZ$15/18 for singles/doubles.

Puaikura Reef Lodge (tel 23-537, telex RG 62045) (11 km, 21.5 km, middle) has 12 modern and well-equipped units. They each have a kitchen and eating area and are wonderful if you're with children as the main sleeping area has a concertina door which you can slide across to shut off the living area (where the kids can sleep). Singles or doubles are NZ$70, extra people cost NZ$15 each, NZ$10 if they're kids. There's also a small swimming pool. The only drawback is that it's very close to the main road although after dark there's very little traffic. The beach, narrow but pleasant and with good swimming, is only a few steps away on the other side of the road.

Dive Rarotonga Hostel (tel 21-873, telex RG 62046), (11.5 km, 21 km, bottom end). Just off the coast road and just beyond the Puaikura Reef Lodge this is the travellers' centre for Rarotonga. There are six twin rooms, one double room and two single rooms, with the singles costing NZ$15 and the other rooms costing NZ$10 per person. The toilets and shower are shared and there's a large communal kitchen with utensils and equipment, a comfortable lounge area and a laundry. The hostel is inconspicuous; there's no sign and you just have to look for the appropriate looking house. Dive Rarotonga, the diving organisers who run the hostel, are on the main road near the Edgewater Motel in Arorangi. They will arrange airport transfers for NZ$2.50.

Lagoon Lodge (tel 22-020, telex RG 62076) (12 km, 20.5 km, middle) is similar in style and situation to the Puaikura Reef. It's also just across the road from the beach, also modern and well kept. At NZ$60/70 for singles/doubles (plus NZ$15 for each extra person or NZ$10 for each extra child) it's also the same price. If there's an advantage it's that it stretches back from rather than along the road so there's less traffic noise. On the other hand the rooms don't have that convenient separation between the sleeping and living (and children) areas. There are 14 rooms and also a small pool.

Several of the rooms are larger two bedroom units – very spacious with a kitchen and living room area, a large verandah and virtually your own private garden. If you've got kids these larger rooms are amongst the best on the island. The larger rooms are NZ$85 for two or three, and the extra charge for the fourth person is NZ$15 (adult) or NZ$12 (child).

Onemura Motel (tel 24-770), (12 km, 20.5 km, middle). This simple place has two self-contained units costing NZ$37.50/43.50 for singles/doubles plus NZ$7 for additional children. There are also two 'tourist flats' which cost NZ$23/28.

Rarotongan Resort Hotel (tel 25-800, telex RG 62003) (12.5 km, 20 km, top end). This 151-room resort is the only 'international standard' hotel in the Cook Islands. It has everything from a seven-day-a-week shop; tennis courts; a swimming pool; a choice of bars, coffee shops and restaurants; it's own beach; a travel centre; to on-the-spot car rental facilities. There's also a business centre with telex, secretarial, photo-copying and fax facilities and even a conference centre although the idea of conferring in the Cooks is a little strange!

The Rarotongan underwent major renovations and upgrading in mid-86 with a major emphasis on giving the hotel a real island feel by using many local craftsmen and acting as a display centre for the best of Polynesian craftsmanship. There are four standards of rooms: standard, super, deluxe and suites. The differences are principally whether you face the garden or the beach, and some variation in equipment levels. Counting up through the grades: singles are NZ$130/150/170/200, doubles NZ$140/160/180/225, triples NZ$150/170/190/250. There is no extra charge for children if they occupy the same room as their parents.

The vast majority of visitors to the Rarotongan are on package deals so these 'rack rates' bear little reality to what people are actually paying. People staying here are more likely to be on a fairly short visit to the Cooks, perhaps part of a quick zip around several Pacific destinations. If you want all mod cons, the feeling of being in a real resort hotel and so on then this could be your place. On the other hand it doesn't have the kitchen facilities and easy living space of the more family oriented motel-style places so if you're here on a longer family vacation you might not find it so convenient.

Orange Grove Lodges (tel 24-770) (15.5 km, 17.5 km, bottom to middle). If you want to economise and really get away from it all then this small lodge (just two rooms) could be just the spot. It's 300 metres back from the beach but set in a beautiful garden with a huge lawn and a stunning mountainscape as a background. The rooms are simple, a little old-fashioned but with everything you could need including cooking facilities. Best of all it's not only cheap (NZ$35/45 for singles/doubles) but you're also invited to help yourself to oranges, grapefruits, lemons, avocados, papayas, bananas and other fruit growing in the garden! One regular visitor likes it so much that he actually books both rooms so he can have it totally to himself!

Palm Grove Lodge (tel 20-002, telex RG 62045) (16 km, 16.5 km, middle). This very pleasant place has just four rooms, in a large garden with a fine stretch of beach right across the road. The rooms are all individual bungalows; the front two rooms are family units with a separate bedroom and room for three or four people. Further back in the grove are two 'island units'. These are just a single room and have some island touches, like a high ceiling, roofed with pandanus. All the rooms are fully equipped with kitchens and equipment and have a verandah in front, and there's a swimming pool. It's a nice place to stay at NZ$55 for singles or doubles, NZ$10 for each extra person.

Moana Sands Resort (tel 26-189, telex RG 62044), (20 km, 12.5 km, middle). Brand new in mid-86 Moana Sands has a two-storey block of rooms, 12 in all, facing directly onto the beach, each with a verandah. The rooms are well equipped, have fridges, tea/coffee making facilities, toaster and electric frypan and cost NZ$75 for singles, doubles or twins, NZ$88 for triples. Six of the rooms are interconnecting. Apart from your own limited cooking facilities there is a restaurant and bar at the motel.

Little Polynesian (tel 24-280, telex 24-280) (20 km, 12.5 km, middle). Only a short distance from the Moana Sands and also right on the beach this longer-established place has nine rooms, all with full kitchen facilities. Two of the rooms are family units with a separate bedroom area. One room is a totally separate 'honeymoon' unit – standing alone, presumably so the occupants can make more noise! There's a swimming pool and rooms cost NZ$65/70 for singles/doubles, NZ$10 for extra people.

Raina Motel (tel 20-197, telex RG 62026) (20.5 km, 12 km, middle). This curious looking three-storey place is right across the road from the beach. There are two family units downstairs with a separate bedroom for two. The upstairs units are smaller, without the separate bedroom, but have the same lounge area, kitchen facilities and so on. Prices are NZ$60 for singles or doubles, NZ$10 for each extra person.

Muri Beachcomber (tel 21-022, telex RG 62055), (23 km, 9.5 km, middle). This popular beachfront place is pleasantly sited on Muri Lagoon, next door to the yacht club. There are regular doubles plus a couple of larger family units with separate bedrooms right beside the swimming pool. Rooms cost NZ$65/70 for singles/doubles plus NZ$10 for each additional person. There are laundry facilities and barbecue areas and the whole place is very new, modern, well kept and well run.

Moana Sunrise (tel 26-560, telex RG 62044), (25 km, 7.5 km, middle). This is a new place just beyond Ngatangiia Harbour with small, modern units right on the beach. The lagoon here is very narrow so swimming is not so good, especially for children, but its not too far to walk back to sheltered Muri Lagoon. Singles or doubles are NZ$55, triples NZ$65, additional children under 12 cost NZ$15.

Ariana Motel (tel 20-521, telex 62036), (29 km, 3.5 km, middle). Situated 200 (uphill) metres off the main road the Ariana Motel has a lush, green garden with a wonderful mountainous backdrop. The eight self-contained rooms are individual bungalows, each with a small balcony, a fully-equipped kitchen and a separate bedroom. There's a pool, barbecue area and a self-service laundry. Costs are NZ$48/54/64 for singles/doubles/ triples. Additional children two to 12 cost NZ$8. One of the rooms is a larger family unit which costs NZ$94 and accommodates up to six people.

Kii Kii Motel (tel 21-937, telex RG 62008), (29.5 km, 3 km, middle). The 20 room Kii Kii is on the beachfront (although the beach here is not so good) and also has a freshwater swimming pool. Room prices for the self-contained units vary from NZ$29/37 for the cheapest rooms through NZ$37/46 up to NZ$48/55 for the beachfront units. Extra adults cost NZ$14, children under 12 NZ$12.

Tamure Resort Hotel (tel 22-415) (30 km, 2.5 km middle). On the eastern edge of Avarua this 35-room waterfront hotel is one of the main entertainment centres on the island. There's entertainment of some form or other four nights a week and the Island Night on Thursday is a major attraction. Otherwise, however, it's no great shakes as a place to stay. In particular the garden areas are overgrown or worn bare, the pool is cloudy and the garden furniture mildewed. It's on the waterfront but the beach here is not the best. Singles are NZ$58, doubles NZ$65, triples NZ$72, additional children from 2 to 12 are NZ$4.

Places to Eat

The widest choice of eating places is found in Avarua although there is also a scattering of places right around the island. Some of the accommodation has dining facilities although many visitors opt to fix their own food for at least some meals. The majority of places to stay have some sort of cooking facilities. See the Places to Stay section and the introductory Food section.

One pleasant surprise with Rarotongan eating is the quality of the local ingredients. Of course a lot of the raw materials (steaks for example) arrive frozen or airfreighted from New Zealand but the locally grown vegetables are excellent. Tomatoes, for example, may not look as technically perfect as you get used to in the USA or Australia but they're certainly tasty.

Avarua If you want cheap snacks or take-away food Avarua is where you'll find it. Right beside the market on the waterfront the *pie van* does burgers, meat pies and other take-away food of the lowest order. It's cheap but little more. *Foodlands*, the major supermarket, has a take-away section where you can get a variety of fairly reasonable pastries, plus sandwiches, meat pies, cold drinks and ice cream.

The *Rarotonga Bakery* makes pretty good bread and also has a selection of pastries, pies, sandwiches and so on. It's probably a small cut up in quality. There's also the *Frosty Boy*, an open-air, fast-food stand in the Cook Islands Trading Company car park. Just beyond the roundabout in Brownes' Arcade

there's *Metua's* (tel 20-850), pleasantly situated on the waterfront although rather hidden away. They do breakfasts and light meals – a good peaceful place for a burger or sandwich at lunchtime.

Avarua also has a number of more expensive restaurants. Right beside the wreck of the *Yankee* is the strangely out-of-place Mexican restaurant *La Cantina*. The food is really quite good, and I certainly had no complaints about the enchiladas which were a meal in themselves. Tacos and other Mexican dishes are NZ$5.50 to 6.50 and other main courses range from NZ$10.50 to 15.50. This is mainly a lunch time place (when it's very popular), at night it can be quite quiet.

Across the road is the *Portofino* (tel 26-480) where the accent is nautical, the food Italian. It's all carried off with with some flair and ability. In fact this place is so popular in the evening that reservations are a very good idea. There's a bar, a surprisingly extensive (and reasonably priced) winelist, starters at NZ$3.50 to 6, good pastas at NZ$7 to 11, main courses at NZ$14 to 18. The fresh fish of the day is usually very good, and so are the desserts. We certainly had no complaints, but it's no problem to spend NZ$60 to 70 for two

with a drink beforehand and coffee afterwards. They also do excellent pizzas both to eat-in and take-away; average prices are NZ$5.50 (small), NZ$9 (medium) and NZ$15.50 (large).

At the same end of town, right on the waterfront at Avarua Harbour, *Trader Jack's* is a brand new seafood restaurant which opened in mid-86.

At the airport end of Avarua *Hibiscus House* (tel 20-823, 4) is a pleasant place with a popular open-air bar. The menu is predominantly Chinese (most dishes NZ$10.50) although there are also some steak or fish-based European dishes at NZ$13 to 16. The food is generally pretty good although one Chinese dish we sampled was far too salty for comfort.

Just before the airport *Romiad's Restaurant* (tel 20-419) is more of a cafe: a place for fish & chips or a burger. Their marinated fish is popular.

Around the Island If you want to eat cheaply you've got a choice between what's available in Avarua or doing your own cooking. The more scattered places are generally more expensive and a major problem with them is that they can be difficult to get to at night unless you've got your own wheels. A number of them get around this by offering to pick you up and take you home after your meal. If you're phoning for reservations (a wise idea) you can check the collection and delivery situation at the same time. Some of the Avarua restaurants also offer transport.

Behind the airport on the Ara Metua, which at this point is a surfaced road, the *Tangaroa Restaurant* (tel 20-017) is a straightforward Chinese restaurant with a bar and take-aways. There are no surprises on the menu – all the standard regulars from chow mein to sweet & sour pork – but it's well prepared and the ingredients (particularly the vegetables) are fresh. Most dishes are NZ$10 to 12. It's open for lunch Monday to Friday, dinner Monday to Saturday.

The *Tumunu Bar & Restaurant* (tel 20-501), next to the Edgewater Motel, has a pleasant outside barbecue area, a straightforward menu with main courses around NZ$12.50 and a popular bar with a cocktail list that includes a 'Long Slow Screw', an 'Orgasm' and a 'Multiple Orgasm'. It makes a 'Tangaroa' sound positively innocuous.

Directly opposite the entrance to the Beach Motel in Arorangi the *Outrigger Restaurant* (tel 27-378) is a relaxed place with moderately expensive but often very good food. Starters are NZ$3 to 6, main courses NZ$13 to 16, desserts around NZ$4. It's licensed and wines costs about NZ$2.50 by the glass, NZ$14 by the carafe. Although the seafood choices are not as extensive as they should be and they often include imports the grilled fish can be excellent and the desserts are simple but delicious. They've also got a children's menu but service can be far too slow for a pleasant meal when children are on hand.

The Rarotongan Resort Hotel (tel 25-800) has several restaurants including the expensive *Brandi's*. It's not really too bad with starters at NZ$3.50 and up, main courses generally around NZ$15 to 20 and desserts around NZ$4. With a bottle of wine for NZ$18 to 20, a drink or two, and some Atiu coffee afterwards a meal for two might cost NZ$75. The food is OK – no award winners but no disasters either. If you think you're going to find some sort of Polynesian high cuisine, however, you'll be disappointed. The wine list is distinctly down-market – Australians will get a laugh out of Seppelts Moyston Claret (a discount-supermarket favourite) at NZ$28 a bottle! The menu was about to get a major revamp soon after we ate there.

Only a couple of km beyond the Rarotongan Resort the *Vaima Restaurant & Bar* (tel 26-123) bills itself as a steakhouse although it actually has a fairly varied menu. Starters are NZ$5 to 7, main courses are NZ$13 to 18 and desserts NZ$4 so it's reasonably expensive. With a couple of drinks beforehand and a bottle of wine (from NZ$16) a complete meal for two can come out to around NZ$75, as expensive as Brandis. The starters and main courses are the best you'll find on Rarotonga – imaginative and well prepared. It's a pity the desserts fall down so disastrously – unless you have an overwhelming love for liqueurs go somewhere else for dessert. Ditto for their special coffees although their regular coffee is fine.

Island Dining

It's indicative of the scale of the Cook Islands that the tourist office's give away booklet boasts that you could stay *10 days* in the Cook Islands and not have to eat at the same restaurant twice! Surprisingly, however, dining out in Rarotonga can be a real pleasure so long as you're willing to spend the money to eat well. So where's the best place if you just one meal on Raro? Well we tried them all and including a bottle of wine (averaging around NZ$16 to 18) and a drink or two beforehand the Rarotongan Resort's up-market *Brandis*, the *Vaima* and the *Portofino* each came out to between NZ$72 and 75 for two. Portofino was the best for overall quality of food and its generally pleasant atmosphere. The Vaima was ´let down by its desserts. Brandis was surprisingly reasonably priced (in comparison to the others that is) given its more expensive appearance. I'd be quite happy to try them all again!

Entertainment

Island Nights Cook Islands dancing is reputed to be the best in Polynesia, superior even to the better known dancing of Tahiti. There are also plenty of chances to see it at the regularly organised 'Island Nights'. There seems to be one on virtually every night of the week. Although the prices hotels quote for their entertainment include meals you can usually get in for the price of a drink or just a small cover charge if you only want to watch.

The *Tamure Resort* is one of the island's major entertainment centres with something on nearly every night.

Their island night is on Thursdays and costs NZ$16.50. They also have shows on Fridays (NZ$17.50) and Saturdays (NZ$18.50) and a *umakai* feast on on Tuesdays. They will organise transport to and from the resort. The Tamure often has special events as well, such as the hotly contested annual contest to find the best dancers in the Cooks. The Edgewater Resort and the Rarotongan Resort also have island nights. The Rarotongan's is probably the best organised and glossiest on the island but you will almost certainly have to pay the full cost, meal and all, and it's necessary to book ahead.

The *Beach Motel* has a Sunday afternoon barbecue which starts at 5 pm and since there's usually very little happening on Rarotonga on a Sunday it's fairly popular. The cost is NZ$12.50 (NZ$7.50 for kids) and, although there may be a little bit of island dancing, entertainment is mainly provided by a Rarotongan pop band playing island music of the strumming guitar variety, and extremely soft western pop.

Pubs, Bars & Discos The *Banana Court Bar* on the main street in Avarua is undoubtedly the best known drinking hole in the Cook Islands, indeed it's one of the best known in the whole South Pacific. There's a disco on Monday and Tuesday, a live band from Wednesday to Saturday. On Friday it stays open late, well into Saturday but on Saturday it shuts at midnight and on church-going Sunday the Banana Court closes down completely. It's a hard-drinking locale but relatively peaceful for all that. The band is quite good and their music is much better than the schmaltz played at so many Rarotongan places. And the audience really gets going. Sure it's just disco-dancing but hips sway and legs quiver like they never do back home! It's great fun.

If you want to kick on till even later then head inland to the *Happy Valley Disco*, just behind Avarua. There are a number of other similar nightclub/discos around Rarotonga.

When it comes to bars the *Beach Bar* at the Beach Motel is popular, not only with the hotel residents. They've got a great selection of beers including Hinano (Tahiti), Vaimo (Samoa), San Miguel (Philippines and other centres), Foster's (Australia) and, of course, a variety of New Zealand beers. Enquire before you drink though, the prices are equally varied. Back a little towards the airport and Avarua the bar at the *Tumunu* is also popular and there's entertainment and a weekly barbecue too.

Other Let's not forget Piri Puruto III who zips up coconut trees and performs other feats most weekday afternoons at various hotels around the island – there's a timetable posted at the bus stop in Avarua. The cost of seeing 'The Master of Disaster' in action is NZ$5.

The Victory and the Empire cinemas are side by side in Avarua and show movies nightly, except Sundays of course. The whole island has been swept by the craze. TV may also arrive soon.

Getting There

See the introductory Getting There section for information on getting to or from Rarotonga from overseas and the Getting Around section for inter-island flights and shipping services within the Cooks. Airline offices are covered in the Information section.

Getting Around

Airport Transport There are taxis and buses at the airport to meet incoming flights. If you opt for bus transport you're very efficiently organised into parties going in various directions, funneled into waiting buses and shot off – all for a fare of NZ$5 per person. If you've prepaid (as well as prebooked) your accommodation it's probable you'll find your transport from the airport is included.

If on the other hand you're a real

shoestringer and think NZ$5 per person is pretty outrageous for travelling five km to, say, Arorangi (it is) you can get together a group and check the taxis (say NZ$1 a km for the whole taxi) or even wait for the hourly public bus (NZ$2 to anywhere). Unfortunately some flights come in at ungodly hours and the public bus only operates during limited hours (see the following section).

Bus There's an island bus service which departs hourly on the hour from the bus stand in the centre of Avarua. It runs right round the coast road in a *counter-clockwise* direction. This means if you're in Arorangi and want to go to Avarua, seven km away, you've got a 25 km trip ahead of you! You can flag the bus down anywhere along its route and the fare is a flat NZ$2. It's a nice way of doing a complete circuit of the island and getting an initial feel for the place. The first departure is at 6 am, the last at 4 pm on weekdays. On Saturdays departures are 7 am to 12 noon. On Sunday, plan to walk! The service seems to run pretty much on time so you can work out relevant arrival times around the island, 10 minutes past the hour in Arorangi for example.

Taxi Taxis are radio-controlled so you can phone for them. They're unmetered but fares are usually around NZ$1 a km. A lot of the taxis are small Japanese minivans and they'll often pick up a couple more passengers going your way and offer you a lower fare.

Rent-a-Car Before you can rent a car or motorcycle you must obtain a local driving licence from the police station in Avarua. It's a straightforward operation taking only a few minutes and costing NZ$2. Even an international permit is not good enough for the Cooks and if your home licence does not include motor-cycles you'll have to pay another NZ$2 and take a practical test. This seems to consist of riding down the road from the

police station, round the roundabout outside the Banana Court and back again without falling off.

You don't need anything very big in Rarotonga - the furthest place you can possibly drive to is half an hour away so the tiny Subaru minicars which are one of the most popular rental vehicles are quite adequate. Subaru seems to have a stranglehold on the Cook Islands car market - every other vehicle is either a Subaru minicar or a Subaru minivan. It's worth phoning around to check the rates as every company seems to have some sort of special rate going. At one extreme there's Budget, the big brother of Cook Islands rent-a-cars, with Subarus at NZ$45 a day, Nissan Marches at NZ$50, Suzuki Sierra jeeps or Nissan Stanzas at NZ$55. They sometimes have long weekend, three-days-for-the-price-of-two deals. Cheaper companies include TPA who has older Honda Civics at NZ$39 a day, and Ace Rent a Car who has small Subarus at NZ$25 a day, slightly larger ones at NZ$37 a day, or NZ$32 a day if you hire for a week.

The main Rarotonga companies are:

Ace Rent a Car (tel 21 902) – Muri
Avis (tel 22-833) – Rarotonga airport
Budget Rent a Car (tel 20 888) – Avarua
Rental Cars (tel 24 442) – Avarua
TPA Rentals (tel 20 611) – Arorangi

There are no surprises for drivers on Raro. The driving is reasonably sane (except late on Friday and Saturday, the two nights when there's heavy drinking) and there's no reason to go fast as there's not far to go wherever you're going. You drive on the left - like in New Zealand, Australia, Japan and much of the Pacific and South-East Asia. There are two rental car rules: don't leave windows open, not because of the risk of theft but because of the chances of an unexpected tropical downpour leaving the car awash; and don't park under coconut palms, because a falling coconut can positively flatten a Subaru 600.

Rent-a-Motorcycle or Bicycle There are lots of motorcycles to rent – usually Yamaha or Honda 50 cc 'step throughs' with automatic clutches; they're very easy to ride. There are one or two places in Avarua that rent them but almost every hotel seems to have a few so you don't have to go far. Costs are usually NZ$10 to 12, possibly with an insurance supplement on day one.

Bicycles are equally readily available and generally cost NZ$5 a day. Again the island is compact enough and the traffic is light enough to make riding a pleasure.

AROUND THE ISLAND

Most island attractions are on or close to the coastal road that encircles Rarotonga. The coast road, a wide, well-surfaced route, is a relatively recent development, although for much of the way around the island it is paralleled by a second road which is slightly inland.

This second road, the *Ara Metua*, follows the path of an ancient Rarotongan road which was originally built of coral blocks. Only traces of the old road remain in an original state as most of it was surfaced or built over during WW II. The WW II construction mainly follows the original route of the ancient road.

Prior to the arrival of missionaries the Rarotongans were scattered inland around the plantations and gardens they tended. The missionaries moved them down to the coast and concentrated them in villages to make them easier to control.

The following description moves around the island counter-clockwise and km distances from the centre of Avarua are indicated. The island is divided up into regions, Puaikura Betela includes Arorangi on the west coast, the south-east part including Titikaveka, Ngatangiia and Matavera is known as Takitumu.

Airport (2.5 km)
The Rarotonga International Airport was officially opened in 1974 and tourism in the Cooks really started at that time.

Cemetery (2.5 km)
Opposite the airport terminal is a small graveyard known locally as the 'brickyard'. A controversial Australian cancer-cure specialist Milan Brych (pronounced 'brick') set himself up in Rarotonga after being chucked out of Australia. When his patron, Cook Islands Prime Minister Sir Albert Henry, was run out of office in 1978, Brych was soon run out of the country as well – he's now in the USA. Cancer patients who died despite his treatment are buried in the graveyard.

Tom Neale, the hermit of Suwarrow atoll, is also buried opposite the airport. He died in 1977 and his grave is in the front corner of the Retired Servicemen's Association cemetery, entered through the gates with the 'Lest We Forget' sign.

Parliament (3.5 km)
The Cook Islands Parliament is just across from the Air Rarotonga terminal. Parliament meets February to March and July to September and so long as you're properly dressed you can watch proceedings from the public gallery. Hours are 1 to 5 pm Monday, Tuesday and Thursday, 9 am to 1 pm Wednesday and Friday.

Golf Course (5.5 km)
At the end of the runway, the Golf Club welcomes visitors to play on its nine-hole course. A round (or two to make it 18) costs NZ$5 and you can also rent a set of clubs for NZ$5 a half day.

Just beyond the golf course is Black Rock where Papeiha is supposed to have swum ashore, clasping the Bible over his head. Actually he was rowed ashore in a small boat! This is also the legendary departure point from where the spirits of the dead are supposed to commence their voyage back to the legendary homeland of Hawaikii. If you follow the road up

Top: Parliament House, Rarotonga (TW)
Bottom: La Cantina Restaurant, Avarua, Rarotonga (TW)

Top: Ascending the final face of Raemaru, Rarotonga (TW)
Left: Tangaroa carving (TW)
Right: Bushwalking on Rarotonga (DC/CITA)

behind the hospital there are good views.

Arorangi (8 km)

Just south of the airport, this was the first missionary built village and was conceived of as a model village for all the others on the island. There are a number of popular places to stay in Arorangi and a couple of popular restaurants. Along the road there are numerous small shops.

The main place of interest in Arorangi is the 1849 CICC church – a large but uninspired building which still has an important role to play in village life. Adjacent to it is the now deserted palace built for the last local ruler by the British. Rising up behind Arorangi is the flat-topped peak of Raemaru. See the walking section which follows for details of the climb.

South Coast (from 12 km)

The south coast of Rarotonga from the Rarotongan Resort right round to the Muri Lagoon has the best beach and the best swimming. The reef is much further out and the sea bottom is relatively free from rocks and sandier than the other beaches. There are lots of good places to stop for a swim, particularly from around the 16 to 20 km mark.

The southern end of the trans-island trek is at about 14.5 km, immediately before the Papua Stream. See the Walking & Climbing section for details. At 16.5 km you can pull off the road beside the beach and park: the beach is very fine here. Just across the road is a sign to the Duncan Bertram Memorial Garden which is half a km off the coast road, on the *Ara Metua*. It's just a pleasant garden where a resident has spent some time cultivating orchids and other local flowers.

Titikaveka (19 km)

There's another picturesque CICC church at Titikaveka with some interesting old headstones in the graveyard.

Muri Lagoon (22 to 25 km)

The reef is further out from the shore on the south side of the island and the Muri Lagoon has the best stretch of beach on the island. The water, though still shallow, has a sandy bottom dotted with countless sea slugs. Out towards the reef are four small islands or *motus*: Taakoka, Koromiri, Oneroa and Motutapu. Taakoka is volcanic, the other islets are sand cays.

The beach on the coast side of Koromiri is particularly popular and at low tide you can easily wade out from the sailing club. Countless hermit crabs scuttle around in the forested undergrowth while offshore on the reef is the rusted hulk of a Japanese tuna fishing boat, the *Iwakuni Maru No 1*. You can wade out to the wreck; the hull has now broken in two and debris litters the reef.

Welland Studio (22 km)

Rick Welland is a personable Californian who has successfully made the seemingly impossible transition from Los Angeles to the Cook Islands. It's hard to imagine two places more diametrically opposed but he's been here for 25 years so he must have managed the change. His paintings capture the people and scenery of Polynesia perfectly – you can see one of them on the title page of this book. Watercolours are generally in the NZ$80 to 120 bracket. It may be advisable to ring first if you want to have a look (tel 23 666).

Rarotonga Sailing Club (23 km)
The sailing club on Muri Lagoon welcomes visitors and has a bar and snack bar upstairs. You can rent canoes for NZ$8 (one person) or NZ$10 (two person) an hour and paddle yourself around the small islands in the shallow lagoon. It's rumoured that the bones of Captain Goodenough's girlfriend are buried near the clubhouse. She was killed and eaten in 1814 while the *Cumberland* was at Rarotonga – see the Rarotongan History section.

Rarotonga Marine Zoo (24 km)
The marine zoo has a large circular tank with a collection of the tropical fish found in the waters around Rarotonga. The prime attractions are the sharks which get a daily feed at 11 am and 2 pm by an intrepid diver. In fact, although they're offered a daily feed they normally eat only every two or three days. The other fish are obviously ravenous at any time and it's quite a sight as the diver is surrounded by a colourful swirl of lunging, darting fish.

The small centre is open Monday to Saturday and admission is NZ$4.50, NZ$2 for five to 12 years old, 50c for kids one to five. The snack bar here has good food.

Ngatangiia Harbour (25 km)
Just north of Motutapu, the northernmost of the four Muri Lagoon islands, is the comparatively wide and deep reef passage into Ngatangiia Harbour. It's a popular mooring spot for visiting yachts. This is also the legendary departure point for the seven Maori canoes which set off around 1350 AD on the great voyage which resulted in the Maori settlement of New Zealand.

Matavera (27.5 km)
The CICC church at Ngatangiia isn't one of the prettiest on the island but the one at Matavera makes up for that. The scenery inland of the stretch of road before Avarua is particularly fine.

Arai-Te-Tonga (30 km)
Just before you arrive back in Avarua a small sign points off the road to the most important *marae* site on the island. Marae were the main religious and ceremonial gathering places of pre-Christian Polynesian society. The marae of a paramount chief or *ariki* was a *koutu* and beside the Ara Metua is a stone marked koutu site – a court where ariki, the great chiefs of pre-missionary Rarotonga, were ceremonially invested with their office. Ceremonial offerings to the ancient gods were also collected here before being placed upon the marae. Arai-Te-Tonga has the remains of an oblong platform four metres long that was at one time over two metres high. At one end stands the 'investiture pillar', a square basalt column two metres high. Don't walk on the marae; its still a sacred site.

Turn left (north-west) along the Ara Metua for about a hundred metres and another sign indicates a stretch of still relatively original road. At one time, perhaps as long as 1500 years ago, the Ara Metua was composed of coral and lava rock along its entire length.

WALKING & CLIMBING
You don't have to get very far into the interior of Rarotonga to realise the population is almost entirely concentrated along the narrow coastal fringe. The mountainous interior is virtually deserted and can be reached only by walking tracks and trails.

The Cook Islands Conservation Service (see the Information section above) puts out a leaflet titled *A Guide to Walks & Climbs* with brief details on a number of interesting walks, some of which are covered in greater detail here. The trail details are very sketchy and the situation is not helped by the little used and indistinct trails. The valley walks are easy strolls suitable for older people or young children but most of the other walks are hard work, often involving difficult scrambling over rocky sections. Apart from the cross island track by the Needle most of the walks are a cross between scaling Everest and hacking your way through the Amazon jungle. Often the views aren't that good either – all you can see is the jungle right in front of your nose.

The interior of Rarotonga is surprisingly mountainous with some steep slopes and sheer drops. It's wise to keep an eye out for these drops as you can stumble across them quite suddenly. Although the trails are often difficult to follow Rarotonga is too small for you to get really lost. You can generally see where you're going or where you've come from. Anyway, following any stream will bring you back down to a coast road.

Walking will generally be easier if you follow the ridges rather than trying to beat your way across the often heavily overgrown slopes. Rarotonga has no wild animals, snakes or poisonous insects but it's wise to wear some sort of leg or ankle protection as you can easily get badly scratched forcing your way through thick brush. Wear running shoes not thongs as the trails can often be quite muddy and slippery. Carry some drinking water too; hiking in Rarotonga can be thirsty work. Walking times quoted are for a round trip from the nearest road access point and do not allow for getting lost – which on most trails is a distinct possibility.

Trans-Island Trek (3 to 4 hours)

The trek across the island via 413-metre Te Rua Manga (The Needle) is the most popular walk on the island. It can also be done as a shorter walk from the north to the Needle and back again rather than continuing all the way to the south coast. Tour companies take parties on this walk.

The road to the starting point runs south from Avatiu Harbour – it's the road running round the back of the airport. The turn-off from this road, which is actually the Ara Metua, is indicated with a sign 'To the Needle'. You can continue easily for about 2.5 km past the power station but then the road begins to deteriorate badly. Unless you're on a motorcycle you're best walking the last km to the starting point which is by a concrete water intake. A sign announces that you're at the start of the Te Rua Manga walking track.

The path is fairly level for about 10 minutes, then it drops down and crosses the Avatiu stream, and then it climbs steeply and steadily all the way to the needle, about a 45-minute walk. If it wasn't for the tangled stairway of tree roots the path would be very slippery in the wet (which it often is). This makes the climb easy but also tiring. At the first sight of the Needle there's a convenient rock to sit on and admire the view. A little further on a sign to 'The Waterfall' indicates the way to the south coast; it's only a short diversion from here to the base of the Needle.

Actually climbing the Needle is strictly for very serious rock climbers – it's high and sheer. You can, however, scramble round the north side to a sheer drop and a breathtaking view from its western edge. From here you can look back down the valley you've ascended from the north coast or look across north-west to the flat peak of Raemaru. You can also see the south coast from the Needle and there are fine views across to Maungatea and Te Kou to the east. Take care on this climb though, there's a long and unprotected drop which would be fatal if you slipped. It's also possible to climb round in the split on the southern side of the Needle but the view is no better and it's a considerably trickier climb.

Retrace your steps to the waterfall sign from where the south coast track drops slightly then climbs to a small peak that gives you get the best view of the Needle you're going to find. From here the track drops slowly down to the south coast, frequently crossing streams and eventually winding back and forth countless times across the Papua Stream. Despite the helpful tree roots this long descent can be annoyingly slippery.

Eventually you get back on to the flat

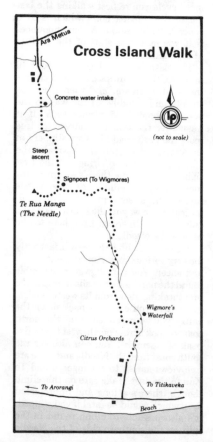

coastal strip right beside the beautiful Wigmore's Waterfall. If you're hot, sweaty and muddy by this time the pool under the fall is a real delight. The sign near the pool warning that the stream is a drinking water supply and that hikers should keep out of it does not apply to the pool as the water intake point is above the waterfall.

From here you're on a vehicle track which brings you back to the coast road in about 15 minutes – passing through coconut and papaya plantations and fields of taro, beans and tomatoes. You emerge on the road via a metal gate with a sign warning that you've just crossed private property, no entry, trespassers prosecuted!

Maungatea (3 to 4 hours)

Maungatea (523 metres) is the peak behind that impressively sheer cliff face directly overlooking Avarua. I did not find this climb particularly interesting and I'm not even sure if I got to the top as it is thickly overgrown and hard to see.

The entry road leads off the Ara Metua and ends just before two houses. You can leave a vehicle and walk straight on in the direction of the road through a small citrus grove and pick up the trail at the other side. The trail crosses the stream a couple of times and then starts to wind up the hill. If it has been raining the trail can be very muddy because of the many pigs around. Island pigs are kept by the simple method of tying a rope from a tree to a front leg. They're fed mainly on coconuts and you'll probably see some pigs – and certainly lots of coconut husks – in this area. Pigs seem to escape fairly regularly so you'll also come across loose ones as well.

The trail starts to climb more steeply and as it does it becomes rather drier, eventually reaching the base of the sheer rock face of Maungatea Bluff. At times the trail seems to simply disappear but all you have to do is keep moving uphill and you'll reach the rock face. Follow the trail

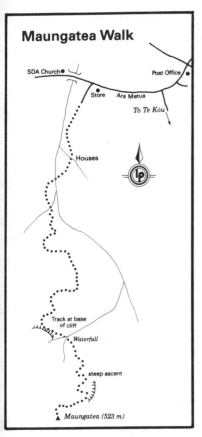

Maungatea Walk

SDA Church●

Post Office ●

Store   Ara Metua

To Te Kou

●Houses

● Track at base of cliff

● *Waterfall*

● steep ascent

▲ *Maungatea (523 m)*

through the ferns, bracken and bush. The ridge is a real knife edge but if you leave it and drop down on the west side it's much too steep and overgrown to get through. Occasionally you get glimpses of Avarua and the north coast at your feet. Looking over the valley from the ridge you have fine views of Ikurangi and Te Manga but mostly you just see dense bush. Whether you're getting close to the top is hard to tell. Perhaps it would be easier to try and hit the ridge top further up towards the summit but without knowing where you're going it's hard to tell.

Coming back down is pleasantly fast, you just slither down the steep slope, grabbing roots and branches as you go.

Te Kou (5 hours)

Te Kou (588 metres) is more or less in the centre of the island and is interesting because there is a crater at the top, indicating Rarotonga's volcanic origins. You can leave a vehicle on the road just before a small group of houses. A track leads off to the left (east) across the river – if you get to the large rectangular water tank you've gone too far. Follow the track until another leads off it to the left (east) and take the left track – don't take the first small foot trail, wait until you get to a wider track (big enough for a small jeep, although it soon becomes narrower).

You soon come out into a valley of taro patches which you have to make your way through by any route you can find. At the far end of the taro patches look for the trail on the right (west) side of the valley. You progress through a dense patch of bush, wading through the river once, and then come into a second narrower valley of taro. At the end of this valley the trail is again to the right side but the valley is narrower and it's easier to find.

From here the trail winds back and forth across the stream and climbs steadily higher. It's fairly easy to follow – overgrown at times but you can always find traces of it. At times it climbs high above the stream but it frequently returns

at the foot of the face round to the left (east) and eventually you'll meet a small waterfall trickling down the middle. Cross the stream and start climbing the hill on the other side. It's very steep but there are plenty of roots and branches to hang onto. Take care, many of them are dead and rotten and break away if you put any weight on them.

Eventually you reach the top of the ridge, also a sheer rock face but facing the Takuvaine Valley. Here your troubles really start because there's no trail at all – you just have to push your way up

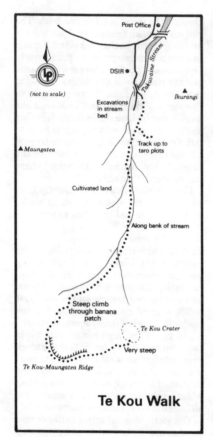

Post Office

DSIR ●

(not to scale)

Tokwaine Stream

▲ *Ikurangi*

Excavations
in stream
bed

Track up to
taro plots

▲ *Maungatea*

Cultivated land

Along bank of stream

Steep climb
through banana
patch

Te Kou Crater

Very steep

Te Kou-Maungatea Ridge

Te Kou Walk

to it until it suddenly heads steeply up the side of the ridge. This is a typical Rarotongan hand over hand climb, hanging on to roots and branches to haul yourself up the hillside. Half way up the trail goes through a banana patch; it's easy to lose the trail but simply keep heading straight up. Eventually you come out on the ridge running between Maungatea and Te Kou.

If you go down the ridge slightly you come to a fallen tree; you can climb out on the trunk and get a fine view across to

Maungatea and down to the north coast. It's worth marking where you reached the ridge so that when you descend from Te Kou you know the point to dive down off the ridge to the stream. The ridge is a real knife edge and there's a fairly distinct trail along it. This is not always the case on Rarotongan walking trails, in fact finding a soft drink can half way up this ridge trail actually felt pleasantly reassuring!

Eventually the trail, which climbs fairly steeply all the way, ends against the final climb to the summit of Te Kou. Here the official leaflet says you have a 'steep climb through bracken to the summit'. And here, for once in my life, I got sensible and gave up. To my mind 'vertical' was a better description than 'steep'. The top disappeared into the clouds and I decided I'd rather have a cold beer! I'd met somebody a few days earlier who had reached the top and he said it was quite spectacular; I wondered afterwards if the best route to the top might not have been further round to the west.

Going down is, as usual, much easier. You slither down the slope from the ridge with great rapidity and finding a way down through the taro swamps is much easier than finding your way up.

Raemaru (3 hours)
Raemaru (351 metres) is the flat-topped peak rising directly behind Arorangi on the west coast. From the coast road you can easily see the route to the top running up a sharp ridge line to the rock face below the final summit area.

Turn off the coast road to the Ara Metua just beyond the Cook Islands Christian Church and then turn right (south) on the Ara Metua. A track (accessible for motorcycles) turns off the Ara Metua to the Te Vai Uri reservoir. Alternatively you can turn off the coast road by the building marked 'Betela' (follow the sign to the White Rose Flats and then turn left (north) on the Ara Metua and take the steep but clear foot

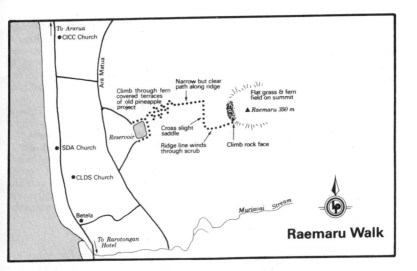

To Ararua
CICC Church

Ara Matua

Narrow but clear
path along ridge

Climb through fern
covered terraces
of old pineapple
project

Flat grass & fern
field on summit

▲ Raemaru 350 m

Reservoir

Cross slight
saddle

SDA Church

Ridge line winds
through scrub

Climb rock face

CLDS Church

Betela

Muriavai Stream

To Rarotongan
Hotel

Raemaru Walk

track which runs up to the south end of the same reservoir.

From the northern end of the reservoir look for trails leading up through the bracken ferns which stretch above the reservoir. These terraced slopes are all that remains of an abandoned project to grow pineapples. The trails are often very indistinct and there are a number of them – you'll often find yourself simply bashing through the brush but you soon come out above this and the way is clear.

A very distinct trail runs up the narrow ridge running directly towards the peak. If you've emerged from the ferns further to the south you'll find yourself on an alternative ridge with a wide, bare trail area along the top. It'll also get you there. On either ridge the trail eventually ends and you then have to turn to the right (south) across a slightly lower saddle to another ridge which takes you right to the rock face of Raemaru. The vegetation here, and indeed all the way to the top, includes ferns but not exclusively as is the case on the lower slopes.

This second ridge trail winds through bush and scrub eventually running right along a sharp edge with fine views down into the Muriavai Valley. The Canterbury Museum in New Zealand has conducted a great deal of research in this valley and found evidence of various early settlements. Eventually the trail ends abruptly at the sheer rock face of Raemaru, well over to the southern edge of the face where it is lower than to the north. This is the hardest part of the climb as you have a tricky scramble up the face to the final plateau. The faint of heart or those who aren't experienced rock climbers may decide to call it a day here. If you press on take care, especially if the rocks are slippery as there's a bit of hanging on by the fingertips and scrabbling for toeholds on the way to the top.

Finally you emerge on an open grassy area which slopes gently to the top. From the far end you can look down across a valley to 519 metre Maungaroa and 413 metre Te Rua Manga, the easily recognised peak on the cross island walk known as The Needle. Looking back you can see along the coast all the way from south of Arorangi to the airport runway in the north.

Ikurangi & Te Manga

The ascent of Ikurangi (485 metres, four hours) and Rarotonga's highest mountain Te Manga (653 metres, five hours) are two of the most difficult on the island. An experienced local guide is probably a necessity if you want to reach the top. The trail to either peak starts from the Ara Metua just to the east of Arau-Te-Tonga (see the Around the Island section).

The track follows the Tupapa stream through taro plots to the point where the Ikurangi trail branches off to the west. Ascending Ikurangi you climb up to the ridge and follow the narrow ridge through the bush moving to the left at the base of the rock summit. There's a steep and tricky climb round the south-west side of the peak then along the ridge to the summit where there are magnificent views.

The Te Manga trail follows the Tupapa stream further inland before branching off along a tributary just beyond a waterfall. The trail goes through plantations of wild bananas, round to the left (east) of a 13-metre waterfall and ascends a ridge marked by a cairn towards the summit. The final ridge to the top is very narrow and steep and great care must be taken.

Valley & Beach Walks

The mountain walks on Rarotonga are hard work. If you want something easier consider the valley walks, such as the stroll along the Avana stream from Ngatangiia. You can drive quite a distance up the road beside the stream and then follow the trail, repeatedly crossing the stream until you reach a pleasant picnic spot at the water intake. A similar walk follows the Turangi stream a little north of Ngatangiia and there is also a trail beside the Muriavai stream in the shadow of Raemaru on the Arorangi side of the island. Be prepared for mosquitoes on these walks.

Any beach on Rarotonga is pleasant for strolling. Start beside Muri Lagoon, for example, and walk towards Titikaveka for fine views of the *motus* on the edge of the lagoon.

A Request

I found the various climbs on Rarotonga rather harder than I'd anticipated. The trails were often difficult to find and then hard to follow. At times it was impossible to know where you were and more than once I failed to reach the final objective of the walk. If you do manage to find better ways up these mountains or have additional suggestions to make – both

Ikurangi & Te Manga Walks

(not to scale)

- Tamure Resort Hotel
- Ara Metua
- Tupapa Stream
- Arai Te Tonga Manae
- Taro
- Taro
- Track follows stream
- Ikurangi
- Ridge
- Waterfall
- Waterfall
- Very Steep
- Te Manga

Top: Cook Islandair flight (TW)
Bottom: Air Rarotonga aircraft at Mangaia Airstrip (TW)

Top: Loading inter-island ships at Avatiu Harbour, Rarotonga (TW)
Left: On board the wreck of the *Yankee*, Avarua, Rarotonga (TW)
Right: Silk & Boyd freighter *Manuvai*, Rarotonga (TW)

Top: Carpenters, Aitutaki, (CITA)
Bottom: CICC church, Arutanga, Aitutaki (TW)

Top: Outrigger on the lagoon, Aitutaki (TW)
Left: Near the Rapae Hotel, Aitutaki (TW)
Right: Signpost, Aitutaki Airport (TW)

about these walks and other possible walks – I'd be very glad to hear them.

OTHER ACTIVITIES

There are plenty of other activities available on Rarotonga from scuba diving (see the Tours section) to golf at the small course near the airport. There's sailing at the Muri Sailing Club or horse riding at Arorangi and Ngatangiia.

Aitutaki

Population: 2335
Area: 18.1 square km

Aitutaki is another Cook Islands entrant in the 'most beautiful island in the Pacific' competition. It's the second largest island in the Cooks in terms of population although in area it only ranks sixth. It's also the second most popular island in terms of tourist visits. The hook-shaped island nestles in a huge triangular lagoon, 12 km across its base and 15 km from top to bottom. The outer reef of the lagoon is dotted with beautiful *motus* (islands) and they're one of the island's major attractions.

Aitutaki also has one of the best 'Island Nights' in the Cook Islands; try to arrange to be on the island on a Friday night to catch this authentic local occasion. Apart from the beaches, motus, snorkelling, fishing and dancing Aitutaki is also historically interesting because this was the first foothold in the Cooks for the London Missionary Society. Only after converting Aitutaki's population did they move on to Rarotonga.

History

Various legends tell of early Polynesian settlers arriving at Aitutaki by canoe but the island's European discoverer was Captain William Bligh on board the *Bounty* on 11 April 1789. The famous mutiny took place just 17 days later as the ship was en route to Tonga. Two years later in May 1791 Captain Edward Edwards came by in *HMS Pandora* searching for those mutineers, and in 1792 Bligh paid his second visit to the island.

In 1814 Captain Goodenough turned up with his ship *Cumberland* after his visit to Rarotonga came to its ill-starred conclusion. He left behind three Rarotongans whom he had taken with him on his sudden departure. In 1821 the missionary John Williams visited Aitutaki briefly and left behind Papeiha and Vahapata, converts from the island of Raiatea near Tahiti, to begin the work of Christianising the Cooks. Williams returned two years later to find Papeiha had made remarkable progress so he was moved on to greater challenges in Rarotonga.

Later European visitors included Charles Darwin on the famous voyage of the *Beagle* in 1835. The first European missionary took up residence in 1839 and the 1850s saw Aitutaki became a favourite port of call for the whaling ships scouring the Pacific at that time. During WW II Aitutaki went through great upheaval when a large American contingent moved in to build the island's two long runways, which until the mid-70s were larger than Rarotonga's airport runway.

Aitutaki suffered from a major hurricane in 1977. At the Rapae Hotel water washed right through the restaurant and kitchen area and the family unit up the hill was turned into an emergency dining room. The CICC church in town, which is well back from the waterfront, also suffered extensive damage.

Information

Cook Islandair and Air Rarotonga both have their offices on the road into the main town Arutanga. There's also a bank on this same road and the Post Office is on the intersection of this road and the road down to the wharf. You can't change money at the Bank but you may be able to at the Post Office! Aitutaki issues it's own special postage stamps which are not available in Rarotonga.

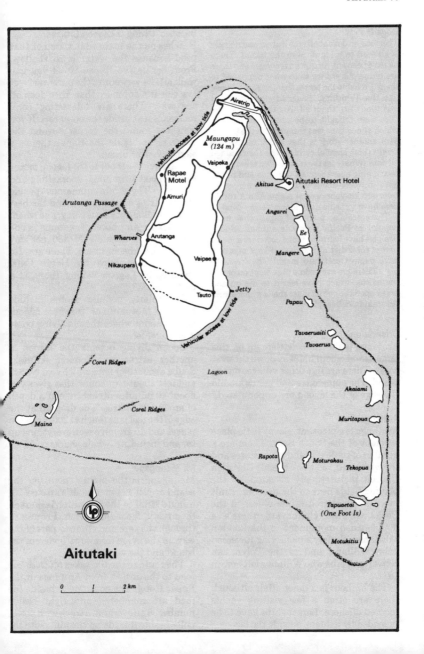

Aitutaki

0   1   2 km

Dogs & Pigs

There are no dogs at all on Aitutaki and nobody is allowed to bring dogs to the island. There haven't been any for quite a few years and there are numerous stories as to what happened to them. Probably the best is that the Aitutakians, like the Tahitians, savoured dog-meat and eventually ate them all. Another is that the dogs were thought to be carriers of leprosy, which at one time was rampant on the island. Still another story is that a dog mauled an *ariki's* (high chief's) child and he then banned all dogs. Whatever the reason it's a relief not to be tripping over them all the time and not to have to worry about your shoes being stolen from outside your door at night. And Aitutaki does have some healthy looking stray cats!

There are also plenty of pigs – that most popular of Pacific domestic animals. South Sea pigs have learnt to make coconuts a major part of their diet although well-kept pigs also have papaya and taro mash! They're tasty pigs. There are even some pigs, kept on one of the motus, which have learnt to dig up and break open the *pahua* clam shells which are an Aitutakian delicacy!

Orientation

Arutanga is the main settlement on this large island, about halfway down the west coast. There are five other villages on the island. The numerous small motus around the edge of the lagoon are unpopulated.

Arutanga

Arutanga is a pleasant, sleepy little place redolent of the South Seas. There are a number of typical island trade stores and the weathered, old Cook Islands Christian Church picturesquely situated by the playing fields next to the harbour. Built in 1828 the church is the oldest in the Cooks. In the churchyard there's a double-sided monument to the London Missionary Society's pioneering Reverend John Williams and to the Polynesian convert Papeiha who Williams left here in 1821.

The harbour is a quiet affair although there are often a few visiting yachts moored offshore. Larger ships have to be unloaded by lighters, outside the lagoon.

Beaches, Diving & Lagoon Cruises

Beaches on the main island are not that good because the water is so shallow. From beside the Rapae Hotel you can walk all the way out to the outer reef – at low tide it's not more than knee deep all the way. There are interesting coral rockpools just inside the outer reef. If you continue round the corner beyond the black rocks beside the Rapae there's a slightly better beach.

You have to get out to the lagoon motus to find good swimming, snorkelling and beaches. There are numerous people offering trips on the lagoon and the best way of finding out who is going, and when, is to ask in your hotel. Takapuna is one good local boatman – NZ$30 per day includes a barbecue lunch. There are also lagoon sailing trips on Hobie Cats, operated by Lagoon Sailing Tours, at a cost of NZ$39.

Particularly popular motus include beautiful Motukitiu or 'One Foot Island' and Akaiami where the old flying boats used to refuel.

Scuba diving outside the lagoon is another attraction. Contact Aitutaki Scuba about their trips which cost NZ$40 and last about two hours; that gives you about 40 minutes diving time at a depth of around 25 metres. The drop-off at the edge of the reef is as much as 200 metres in places and divers have seen everything up to, and including, whale sharks.

Mt Maungapu

Maungapu is the highest point on the island at just 124 metres. It's an easy 20-minute stroll to the top which is marked by a rusty, fenced-off pylon. I squeezed through the gate and climbed part of the way up the pylon for a superb view of the island and the whole lagoon.

The route to the top takes off from the road to the airport from Arutanga or the Rapae Hotel. The power poles beside the road are numbered and right beside number 38 an overgrown track with power poles beside it leads up the hill. Note the playhouse made out of the forward fuselage of an old DC-3 in the back garden of the house beside pole number 27.

Around the Island

You can do a complete circular tour of the island, even on a pushbike, in a couple of hours. The road runs close to the coast most of the way although only in Arutanga itself is it surfaced. There are a handful of small villages apart from the main town.

The golf course out by the airport is notable for one hole which plays across the runway! Play has to stop when aircraft arrive.

The Coral Route

Aitutaki had a pioneering role in Pacific aviation as a stopping point in Tasman Empire Air Line's 'Coral Route'. Back in the 1950s TEAL, the predecessor to Air New Zealand, flew across the Pacific: Auckland-Suva (Fiji)-Apia (Western Samoa)-Aitutaki-Papeete (Tahiti). The first leg to Suva was flown by DC-6s but the rest of the way was by four-engined Solent flying boats.

The stop at Aitutaki was purely to refuel, indeed this was carried out at the uninhabited motu of Akaiami. It took over two hours so passengers had a chance to take a swim in the lagoon. Flying in those days was hardly a one stop operation: one day took you from Suva to Apia and the next day required a pre-dawn departure from Apia in order to make Papeete before nightfall. The flying boats were unpressurised so they did not fly above 3000 metres and they sometimes had to descend to less than 500 metres.

The old Solents carried their 60-odd passengers in seven separate cabins and in some degree of luxury. Food was actually cooked on the aircraft, in contrast to today's reheated airline meals. At that time the fortnightly flight into Papeete was the only direct air link between Tahiti and the rest of the world and the aircraft's arrival was a major event.

Usually the trips were uneventful but on one occasion a malfunction at Aitutaki required off-loading the passengers while the aircraft limped on to Tahiti on three engines. It was a week before it arrived back to collect the

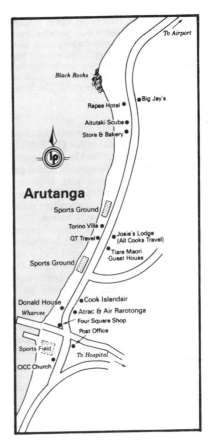

passengers – who by that time had begun to really enjoy their enforced stay on hotel-less Aitutaki. On another occasion the aircraft was forced to return to Aitutaki when the Tahiti lagoon turned out to be full of logs. The trip to Tahiti was attempted twice more before the lagoon was clear enough for a landing. One of the TEAL flying boats is now on display in the transport museum in Auckland, New Zealand.

Solents were also used by British Airways (BOAC in those days) on routes from England through to India and Australia. A couple were still in use by Ansett Airlines in Australia for Sydney-Lord Howe Island flights right into the early '70s, but flying boat travel was really ended by WW II. Prior to the war most long-range commercial flights were made by flying boats as suitable airports for long-range land planes did not exist. After the war not only had large, long-range aircraft been greatly improved but there were airport runways capable of handling them all over the world. The flying boat days were over.

Places to Stay

The popular and pleasantly situated *Rapae Cottage Hotel* (telex HY 2002) is set in lush gardens beside the lagoon, about two km from the centre of Arutanga. The orange hotel cats and a motley collection of chickens (at least one rooster per room commented one visitor) roam the grounds. There are 13 rooms, 12 of them doubles in duplex units – they're simple but comfortable with bathroom, tea/coffee making equipment and a big shady verandah. Singles/doubles are NZ\$49/54. The 13th room is a family unit which occupies the same space as a regular duplex. It's equally spartan, has beds for six people (they allow for large families) and a kitchen. The family unit costs NZ\$64 for two people, additional people cost NZ\$5 each and children under five are free.

There are a number of guest houses in Aitutaki, most of them along the road between the Rapae Hotel and the centre of Arutanga. They offer much the same facilities and standards – a simple room with common bathroom facilities. Prices are all pretty similar too. The *Tiare Maori Guesthouse* has six rooms and costs NZ\$25/40 including breakfast and charges NZ\$10 for dinner. *Josie's Lodge* is a pleasant place at NZ\$25/35 including breakfast, with dinner at NZ\$10 again. Other places include *Torino Villa* across the road from the Tiare Maori and Josie's and the *Aitutaki Guest House* which is further on beyond the centre.

At the far end of the airstrip the *Aitutaki Resort Hotel* (tel 20-234 in Rarotonga, telex RG 62048) is built on Akitua motu, now joined to the main island by a causeway. There are 25

Tapairu, abducted to Aitutaki by Capt Goodenough

individual, twin-bed cottages and the resort has all mod cons including a swimming pool. Nearly everybody staying here will be on some sort of all-inclusive package deal; singles cost NZ\$122 to 142, doubles NZ\$122 to 182. The major drawback, apart from the prices, is the resort's considerable isolation from the rest of the island.

Places to Eat

The restaurant at the *Rapae Hotel* has good food – their home-cured ham sandwiches are delicious and they have meals for NZ\$8 to 10. On Friday night they have their excellent Island Night Buffet (NZ\$14.50) and on Sunday night they have a barbecue (NZ\$13.30). *Big Jay's* has fish & chips for NZ\$4 and other light snacks but basically it's a place for entertainment. If you want to go out to the *Aitutaki Resort* for dinner they'll send their bus for you.

The stores have the usual Cook Islands selection of tins and the usual limited variety of fresh fruit and vegetables. The choice is more restricted than on Rarotonga and the prices are higher. It's worth bringing some supplies with you, particularly if you plan to cook for yourself, although the Rapae Hotel's family room is virtually the only place with cooking facilities.

The shop next to Aitutaki Scuba, near the Rapae Hotel, has excellent fresh-baked bread. Aitutaki's large lagoon supplies the best variety of fresh fish in the islands but you've got to catch them yourself or know somebody who has been fishing! If you go on a lagoon cruise you're likely to come back with some.

Entertainment

Island Night at the *Rapae Hotel* on Friday night is a social event only out-done by the Sunday church service. There's a buffet served from around 7.30 pm which costs NZ$14.50 and provides a varied spread of island specialities from octopus to roast pork, fried fish to taro, curried goat to clams. Eating here, or simply being a Rapae Hotel guest, also gets you a ringside seat but if you don't want to eat there's no cover charge or entry cost.

The band starts playing around 8 pm and the dancing gets under way around 9.30 pm. It's an hour of raucous fun. Large matrons return from the bar through the dancers and show very clearly that they can still swing a hip as well as any upstart teenager! The finale involves pulling *papa'a* out of the audience and getting them to show what they've learnt. By this time most people have had enough to drink for embarrassment to be minimal. The band continues on until midnight with an increasingly unsteady but highly entertaining crowd.

Big Jay's also has entertainment – a local band and dancers – on Thursday, Friday and Saturday nights. The entry charge is only NZ$1 and drinks are reasonably priced.

Getting There

Air Aitutaki was the first outer island in the Cooks to have regular air links with Rarotonga. There are two flights a day (except on Sundays) with Cook Islandair and with Air Rarotonga. Round trip fares are NZ$148 with Cook Islandair, NZ$190 with Air Rarotonga. See the introductory Getting Around section for details on discounts.

Aitutaki's large airstrip was built by USA forces during WW II. It's the only airport in the Cooks with a two-way runway and it could handle much larger aircraft than those currently used. You could fly Boeing 737s into Aitutaki.

Ship Fares from Rarotonga on Silk & Boyd ships are NZ$30.80 deck class, NZ$60 cabin class. Although Aitutaki is a popular yachting destination the narrow reef passage is too hazardous for large ships to enter so cargo is normally taken by lighters outside the reef.

Getting Around

A minibus meets the flights and charges NZ$3 into town. Around the island there's a reasonable network of roads although apart from a km or two through Arutanga none of them are paved. They're not too rough and you can hire motorcycles (NZ$10 to 12 a day) or pushbikes (NZ$5 a day) to get around. For some reason there seems to be a shortage of motorcycles; if you have to have one then it may be an idea to organise one in advance. The Rapae Hotel, Big Jay's and other places rent them. There are also a handful of cars to rent although there aren't many four-wheeled vehicles on the island. Aitutaki is small enough to explore on a pushbike.

Manuae

Population: 12
Area: 6.2 square km

The two tiny islets of Manuae and Te Au

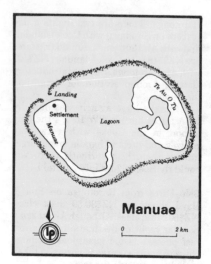

Manuae

0   2 km

the only parts of a huge volcanic cone which break the surface. The cone is 56 km from east to west, 24 km north to south. The other highpoint on the rim of this vast cone is the Astronomer Bank, 13 km west of Manuae. It comes to within 300 metres of the ocean's surface. Manuae is 101 km from Aitutaki and coconuts were often collected from the atoll by Aitutakians.

History
Cook was the European discoverer of the atoll. He sighted it in 1773 during his second voyage and in 1777 on his third voyage he paused to investigate but did not land. The islands were named the Hervey Islands by Captain Cook, a name which for a time was applied to the whole southern group, but fortunately that name is rarely used.

In 1823 the missionary John Williams visited the island and there were about 60 inhabitants. There were only a dozen or so in the late 1820s and the missionaries took them to Aitutaki. Later a series of Europeans made temporary homes. The the best known was the prolific William Marsters who in 1863 was moved to Palmerston with his three wives. Today, that island's entire population is descended from him.

O Tu are effectively unpopulated – occasionally copra cutting parties visit from Aitutaki. Perhaps there were copra-cutters on the island at the time of the 1981 census. The Cook Islands Government has suggested that in view of the unspoilt nature of the lagoon the islands should be declared an international marine park.

The two islets of Manuae are actually

Atiu & Takutea

Atiu

Population: 1225
Area: 26.9 square km

The third largest of the Cook Islands, Atiu is noted for its raised coral reef or *makatea*, a phenomenon also found on the islands of Mangaia, Mauke and Mitiaro. The island has had a colourful and bloodthirsty history as the Atiuans were the warriors of the Cooks and specialised in creating havoc on all their neighbouring islands.

Unlike all the other Cook Islands, including Mangaia with its similar geography, the villages in Atiu are not on the coast. The five villages – Areora, Ngatiarua, Teenui, Mapumai and Tengatangi – are all close together in the centre of the hill region. When the missionaries moved the original settlements together they effectively created a single village – the post office and church form the centre, and the 'villages' radiate out from this centre on five roads, like the five arms of a starfish.

Atiu is surprisingly interesting for the visitor – there are some fine beaches, magnificent scenery, excellent walks, ancient *marae* (pre-Christian ceremonial and religious sites) and the makatea is riddled with limestone caves, some of them used as ancient burial caves. You can also see coffee production, sample pineapples and there's an excellent place to stay. Most people stay two days, the usual time between flights, and that really isn't long enough. Atiu is not, however, a place for easy lazing around – you have to get out and do things, burn some energy. This was one of my favourite places in the Cooks and the island really deserves more visitors!

Geology

Atiu's geology is fascinating. It's thought that Atiu rose out of the sea as a volcano cone around 11 million years ago. The cone was worn down to a shoal, then upheaval (or a drop in the sea level) raised the shoal to form a flat-topped island. Further eons produced a wide coral reef around the island but then, about 100,000 years ago, the island rose another 20 or so metres out of the sea. The coral reef then became a coastal plain, stretching back about a km from the new coastline to the older central hills. In the past 100,000 years a new coral reef has grown up around most of the island, but this is only a hundred or so metres wide.

The island today is rather like a very low-brimmed hat with a flat outer rim. This outer rim or makatea is principally rough and rugged, fossilised coral.

Atiu Cross Section

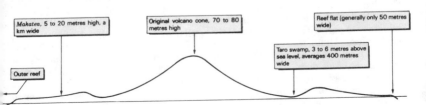

Makatea, 5 to 20 metres high, a km wide

Original volcano cone, 70 to 80 metres high

Reef flat (generally only 50 metres wide)

Taro swamp, 3 to 6 metres above sea level, averages 400 metres wide

Outer reef

Although it's comparatively infertile the makatea is no barren wasteland; it's a veritable jungle, densely covered in scrub and coconut palms. The makatea starts off around five metres in depth right at the coast and gradually slopes up to around 20 metres at its inner edge. Then instead of sloping up immediately into the central hills – the old volcanic core – there's a circular band of swamp. It seems that water running off the hills permeates the edge of the makatea and has eroded it away to form this damp swamp area. It's extensively used for taro cultivation but it's also a breeding ground for mosquitoes! Inland from the swamp is the inner plateau, the most fertile area of the island where coffee and pineapples are grown.

History

Atiu was once known as Enua-manu which can be translated as 'land of birds' or 'land of insects'. Numerous legends tell of early settlers arriving by canoe or of visits by legendary Polynesian navigators. What is more certain is that some time before the first European arrival three *ariki* controlled the island and began to extend their power over the neighbouring islands of Mauke and Mitiaro.

The European discovery of Atiu is credited to Captain Cook on 3 April 1777. The previous day the Atiuans had made friendly visits to his ships the *Resolution* and *Discovery*. The Atiuans were uninterested in any items they were offered for trade but they did want a dog. They had heard of but not seen such an animal and Cook would have been happy to oblige them for, 'We had a Dog and a bitch on board belonging to one of the Gentlemen, that were a great nusence in the Ship', but the gentleman was reluctant to part with them. Fortunately the Tahitian, Omai, who Cook had taken back to England on his previous voyage, offered one of his dogs.

The next day the captain sent three of his boats ashore to try to procure supplies. His men spent a long day being feted (and

Atiu Crest of Identity

pickpocketed) by the Atiuans – they watched wrestling matches and dancing displays – but came back effectively empty handed. At one point when a large oven was being prepared Omai was so frightened it was intended for himself and his companions that he came straight out and asked the Atiuans if they were preparing to eat them! The Atiuans expressed shock at the mere thought of such an idea but subsequent tales of the Atiuans' eating habits amongst the people of Mauke and Mitiaro makes one wonder about their ingenuousness.

His men safely back on board, Cook 'resolved to try no more and thought my self well off that it ended as it did'. He sailed away and managed to find the necessary provisions, principally for the cattle he had on board, on the neighbouring island of Takutea, where he left 'a hatchet and some nails to the full Value of what we took from the island'.

Forty years were to pass before the next European contact when in late 1822 or early 1823 two Polynesian 'teachers' were sent from Bora Bora near Tahiti. They were singularly unsuccessful although when the Reverend John Williams turned up a few months later searching for Rarotonga, he quickly persuaded the Atiuans to take the first steps of burning their 'idols', destroying their marae and starting work on a church. The missionaries subsequently made occasional visits from Tahiti but in 1836 the Tahitian convert Papeiha was sent from Rarotonga and started the serious work of Christianising the island.

Williams' visit in 1823 and the subsequent conversion of the inhabitants of the neighbouring island of Mauke had a macabre sidelight. Some time before his visit a dispute had evolved between Atiu and Mauke. Rongomatane, the leading Atiuan chief, had rushed off to Mauke bent on revenge and virtually wiped out the islands' inhabitants. Having killed, cooked, and eaten their fill the Atiuans took back canoe-loads of cooked Maukeans for the rest of the Atiuans to sample.

This was not the first time Rongomatane had descended upon Mauke, and the Atiuans had also worked off their appetites on the unfortunate inhabitants of Mitiaro. One of Williams' first converts in Atiu was none other than this bloodthirsty cannibal chief. Shortly after, Williams and his new Christian convert turned up on Mauke; it's hardly surprising that the poor inhabitants of the island embraced Christianity with such alacrity and fervour!

Information

There's electricity for 12 hours a day, running in the evening until midnight, starting up again in the early morning and also running for a period in the early afternoon. Atiu produces two important crops although both face numerous problems. Pineapples are grown and exported fresh to New Zealand. Coffee is also grown; the only commercially grown coffee in the Cook Islands.

Two important items to bring with you to Atiu are a torch (flashlight) and mosquito repellent. The Atiu Motel lends you a torch for cave exploring but you'll want a backup in case of emergencies when underground. And the mosquitoes in the swamp region are voracious and exceedingly numerous. At times you seem to have such a line of them across any tasty looking stretch of skin there seems to be no room for a single additional freeloader. Leave your restaurant gear behind in Raro, on Atiu you need old T-shirts, torn shorts, worn-out running shoes. Be prepared to get muddy, sweaty and tired!

If you want more information on Atiu there are a couple of interesting books to look for. *Atiu through European Eyes* (Institute of Pacific Studies, University of the South Pacific, 1982) is fascinating. It's subtitled 'A Selection of Historical Documents 1777-1967' and is a collection of references to Atiu from books and reports, reproduced in facsimile form. There are three sections: 'explorers' is principally from the logbook for Cook's visit in 1777; 'missionaries and traders' has accounts of Atiu by those early visitors; and the third section includes more modern academic reports on Atiu's archaeology, its fascinating geology and various customs and social systems. Also published by the Institute of Pacific Studies *Atiu, an Island Community* (1984) is a modern study of Atiu's current conditions and customs.

Beaches & Coast

Atiu is not a great place for swimming – the surrounding lagoon is rarely more than 50 metres wide and the water is generally too shallow for more than wading and gentle splashing around. There are, however, countless beautiful, sandy bays all along the coast. You can easily find one to yourself and when you tire of sunbathing just slip into the water for a cooling dip. Some of them are easily reached but to get to others a little pushing through the brush is required, although the coastal roads are rarely more than 100 metres from the coast.

On the west coast Orovaru Beach is thought to be where Cook's party made their historic landing. There's a large rock in the water just off the beach. Further south is the longer sweep of Taungaroro Beach, backed by high cliffs and sloping fairly steeply into the water. South again is Tumai Beach and there are plenty of others. The coast road runs all the way down to Te Tau at the southern tip. The water at Taunganui Harbour is clear and deep enough for good swimming and snorkelling.

The south-east coast takes the brunt of the prevailing northerly winds and the sea, washing fiercely over the reef, is often unsafe for swimming. There are, however, a series of picturesque little beaches including Matai at the start of the south-east coast road and Oneroa at the end. About halfway along this road is the turn-off to Takauroa Beach, just by a stretch of old pig fence. If you walk back along the rugged cliff face about a hundred metres there are some sink holes deep enough for good snorkelling. They are only safe at low tide or when the sea is calm.

On the north-east coast there's a km-long stretch where there is no fringing reef and the sea beats directly on the cliffs. At the end of the road Tarapaku is a rarely used emergency boat landing and there's a pleasant stretch of beach. There are more beaches south to Oneroa but there is no coast road.

Caves

The makatea is riddled with limestone caves, complete with stalactites and stalagmites. You'll stumble across many small ones in any ramble through the makatea so take a torch (flashlight). Take your bearings too as it's very easy to get totally confused underground and when (if?) you finally find your way out it may be by a different exit.

It's necessary to take a guide (usually about NZ$10 plus a small charge for each additional person) partly because the caves can be difficult to find but also

because most of the better known caves are on 'owned' land and permission must be obtained before you enter. Many of the caves were used for burials although when and why nobody knows. If you visit one of these caves do not move or take any of the bones. At the very least there will be a curse on you if you do!

The Te ana o Raka burial cave is one cave you can visit by yourself. You can approach it either by taking the road down from the central plateau or by taking the road which runs inland from about three quarters of the way down the airstrip. The cave is just off the road and very easy to find. There are, however, numerous entrances and exits to this extensive cave and it is very easy to get confused.

In the south-east of the island is the Anatakitaki or 'cave of the kopeka'. The cave is reached by a longish walk across the makatea from the plateau road. Kopekas are tiny birds, very much like swifts, which nest in huge numbers inside the cave. When they come out to hunt insects they are never seen to land, only in the cave do they rest. Inside the pitch dark cave they make a continuous chattering, clicking noise which they use to find their way around like bats. Try to dissuade your guide from catching the birds, a trick they perform by throwing a shirt or jacket over the sleeping birds on the roof of the cavern. Some of the chambers in this extensive cavern are very large. Although this is the main kopeka cave they do nest in smaller numbers in at least one other cave. There's a legend that relates how a Polynesian hero, Rangi, was led to this cave which concealed his missing wife, by a kingfisher bird.

In the south-west the Rima Rau burial cave is a smaller cave reached by a vertical pothole. There are many bones to be seen in this cave and nearby there's a very deep sink hole with a deep, cold pool at the bottom.

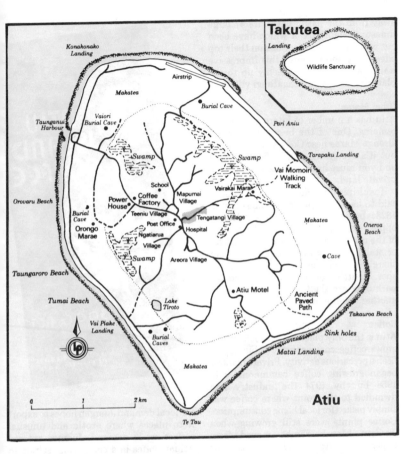

Takutea

Landing

Wildlife Sanctuary

Konakonako Landing

Makatea

Airstrip

Burial Cave

Taunganui Harbour

Vaiori Burial Cave

Pari Aniu

Swamp

Swamp

Tarapaku Landing

Vai Momoiri Walking Track

Orovaru Beach

School

Coffee Factory

Power House

Teeniu Village

Mapumai Village

Vairakai Marae

Makatea

Oneroa Beach

Burial Cave

Orongo Marae

Post Office

Ngatiarua Village

Tengatangi Village

Hospital

Taungaroro Beach

Swamp

Areora Village

Cave

Tumai Beach

Lake Tiroto

Atiu Motel

Ancient Paved Path

Vai Piake Landing

Burial Caves

Takauroa Beach

Sink holes

Matai Landing

Makatea

Atiu

0   1   2 km

Te Tau

Vai Momoiri Track & Vairakai Marae

From Tarapaku Landing on the north-east coast a walking track leads inland all the way to the central villages. It's best to arrange transport round to the Landing so you can walk the whole way inland. At first the track winds across a wonderful stretch of makatea with thick vegetation, colourful flowers and impressive outcrops. Much of the track is paved with stone slabs and there are numerous small caves very close to the path. At one point you can see the Vai Momoiri, a deep canyon off the track to the left, filled with brown water. A short stretch of tunnel connects this water to a second, similar sink hole.

Eventually the path heads into the swamp and if the log bridge has not been repaired you may have to wade through knee-deep water and mud for about 100 metres before reaching drier ground. The path follows irrigation ditches and at one point turns sharply across a cement culvert. Look to your left at this point to the 37-metre-long wall of the Vairakai Marae. It's somewhat overgrown but stands parallel to and only a metre or so away from the path. There are 47 large limestone slabs, six of which have been cut with curious projections on their top edge. Very shortly after this impressive wall the path climbs steeply up to the plateau and enters Tengatangi village.

Other Marae

Atiu has a number of interesting marae remains. One of the best known is the Orongo Marae near Cook's landing place but it's overgrown and difficult to find and you must have a guide since it's on private land.

Teapiripiri Marae where Papeiha is said to have first preached the gospel in 1823 is behind the tennis courts and house opposite the Post Office. There's little left of the marae apart from some stalactites or stalagmites lying on the ground but there's a memorial stone to mark the spot. A little north of here, behind the park opposite the CICC church, there's another small marae.

Coffee

Atiu is the only place in the Cooks which grows coffee commercially – but it has been a precarious activity. Private planters began growing coffee commercially in 1958 but by 1974 the industry had dwindled to the point where coffee was simply picked for local home consumption. Coffee plants were still growing when Juergen Manske-Eimke moved from Nigeria to Atiu and changed his occupation from construction engineer to coffee grower. The Atiu coffee business is now rebounding and Juergen hopes that the three tons of coffee the island currently produces annually will expand to twice that level. At present there's about eight hectares of coffee being grown but that could potentially be expanded to around 25 hectares. The supermarkets and fancier restaurants of Rarotonga alone can use about 3½ tons of coffee a year, more than Atiu is currently producing.

When coffee production expands beyond

the local demand Juergen hopes to export it to places where exotic and unusual coffees are in demand. Juergen entered Atiuan coffee in a coffee competition in Hawaii recently (Atiuan coffee is similar to the renowned Hawaiian Kona) and it came third out of 16 entrants. The coffee is usually picked from February to May. Because of the small scale of production and relatively low labour costs Atiuan coffee is 100% sun dried and 100% hand selected. Coffee growing in Atiu has its problems – wild pigs, too much sunshine, and the perennial Cook Islands land-ownership questions all cause hassles. It's good coffee though, and you can buy a half kg package from the factory for NZ$7.50 (NZ$10 in Rarotonga shops).

Juergen gives tours of the coffee plantations, pulping factory and the new factory where it's hulled, roasted and packed. They cost NZ$10 (additional people NZ$5). The tour ends with a cup (or two) of Atiuan coffee. His wife Andrea is a textile designer and the Atiuan coffee package is her work.

Other

There are a couple of dusty display cases with some Atiuan artefacts in the library of Atiu College. The CICC church in the centre of the villages has walls over a metre thick and is in the traditional island style.

The villages have a surprising number of tennis courts – a few years ago the five villages got into a tennis court building competition, each attempting to build a better one than the next!

Lake Tiroto is noted for its eels which are a popular island delicacy. On the western side of the lake is a cave which leads right through the makatea to the sea. You can crawl through it for a considerable distance if the water in the lake is low enough. Be prepared to get very muddy, however. And watch out for eels.

Bush Beer Schools

Don't miss the opportunity to visit a *tumunu* while you're in Atiu. It's a direct descendant of the old *kava* ceremony of pre-missionary times. *Kava* was a drink prepared from the root of the pepper plant *piper methysticum*. It was not alcoholic but it certainly had an effect on its drinkers – ranging from a mildly fuzzy head to total unconsciousness! Drinking *kava* was always a communal activity with some ceremony involved; you could not be a solitary *kava* drinker. In Fiji *kava* is still popular today but in the Cook Islands the missionaries managed to all but totally stamp it out. During that missionary period, however, when drinking was banned, the *tumunu* came into existence and men would retreat to the bush to drink home-brewed 'orange beer'. The 'tumunu' is the hollowed out coconut palm stump which was traditionally used as a container for brewing the beer.

Tumunu are still held regularly at various places on the island although the container is likely to be plastic these days and the beer will be made from imported hops, much like any western home brew, rather than from oranges as in the old days. Technically, however, the bush beer schools are still illegal. If you stay at the Atiu Motel, Roger will arrange an invitation for a visit to the local *tumunu*; men only, though.

There's still quite a tradition to the beer schools. The barman sits behind the *tumunu* and ladles the beer out in a coconut cup. Each drinker swallows his cup in a single gulp and returns the empty cup to the barman who fills it for the next in line. You can pass if you want to but by the end of the evening everybody is decidedly unsteady on their feet. Including, on the night I went, the barman who is supposed to stay sober and keep everyone in line! At some point in the evening the barman calls the school to order by tapping on the side of the *tumunu* with the empty cup and then says a short prayer. As a visitor to the *tumunu* you should bring a kilo of sugar or a couple of dollars, the equivalent in cash.

Places to Stay & Eat

The *Atiu Motel* is the only organised accommodation on the island. Roger and Kura Malcolm have three units at NZ$32/38/44 for singles/doubles/triples. They're delightful, individual, A-frame chalets that make maximum use of local materials. The main beams are sections of coconut palm trunks retaining the outer bark. Coconut palm wood is used extensively inside (it's a beautiful wood) and drawer and cupboard fronts are made with hibiscus wood. So much of the accommodation in Rarotonga makes absolutely zero use of local materials and has no 'Pacific' feel at all; this place should be a real object lesson.

The rooms have a single and double bed and on top of the bathroom there's a mezzanine area where you could sleep another person or two. There's a verandah in front and a kitchen area. There is no place to eat on Atiu so you have to fix your own food – each unit comes with a fridge and cupboard full of food and at the end of your stay you're simply billed for what you've used.

The Atiu Motel is a great place to stay and Roger is helpful and informative. Should it be full up you could no doubt find a place to stay with one of the villagers. Roger could probably suggest something. Air Rarotonga or Cook Islandair will book you a room at the Atiu Motel.

There are a several trade stores on Atiu and two bread bakers and three places that bake donuts. The amount of bread produced is quite amazing, as on all the islands. Donuts are supplied on a loop made from a strip of leaf and you can hang it from the handlebar of your motorcycle and ride off. *Maroro* or flying fish are an Atiuan delicacy; they're caught in butterfly nets on full moon nights during the spawning season.

Getting There

Air Rarotonga and Cook Islandair fly to Atiu about three times a week each. The 40 minute flight costs NZ$85 with Air Raro. The airport is on the north-east corner of the island. It was only built there in '83 as the old airstrip, itself built only in '77, was too small. The new strip's coral surface is also better. Roger Malcolm from the Atiu Motel meets incoming guests and drops off outgoing ones.

Silk & Boyd also sail here. The all weather harbour at Taunganui was built in 1974 but it's still too small to take ships so they have to be unloaded onto a barge while they're standing offshore. Prior to '74 getting ashore on Atiu could be a pretty fraught business. In fact some say the Atiuans, once the terror of Mauke and Mitiaro, could have been the terror of

many more places were it not for their lack of harbour facilities. As it was the Atiuans could never build really big ocean-going canoes. Instead they used smaller canoes and once offshore lashed two together to make a larger and more stable vessel.

Getting Around

Atiu is great for walking but you definitely need a motorcycle to get around – the Atiu Motel rents motorcycles for NZ$12 a day. Take great care when walking across the makatea. The coral is sharp as hell. It's often like walking across razor blades and if you slipped and fell you'd be sliced to pieces. Wear good shoes too; if you stubbed your toe while wearing thongs you'd probably cut it right off.

Takutea

Population: unpopulated
Area: 1.2 square km

Clearly visible from Atiu this small sand cay is only six metres above sea level at its highest point. The island has also been called Enua-iti which simply means 'small island'. Cook visited Takutea in 1777, shortly after he left Atiu, and paused to search for food for the livestock on his ship.

It's only 16 km north-west of Atiu and copra collecting parties used to come from that island. Today it is unpopulated and rarely visited. Many seabirds including frigates and tropic birds nest on the island.

Top: Vairakai Marae, Atiu (TW)
Left: Crossing the *makatea*, Atiu (TW)
Right: Entrance to Anatokitaki Cave, the cave of the *kopeka*, Atiu (TW)

Top: Stalactite or stalagmite from an ancient *marae*, Atiu (TW)
Left: CICC church, Atiu (TW)
Right: Skulls, Rima Rau Burial Cave, Atiu (TW)

Top: Cook Islands Trading Company Store, Oneroa, Mangaia (TW)
Left: Northern view from Rangimotia, Mangaia (TW)
Right: Fishing from the reef, Mangaia (TW)

Top: Stalagmites in Teruarere Cave, *Mangaia* (TW)
Bottom: View from the central highlands to the edge of the *makatea*, Mangaia (TW)

Mangaia

Population: 1360
Area: 51.8 square km

The second largest of the Cook Islands, Mangaia is not much smaller than Rarotonga although its population is much smaller and has declined sharply in recent years. The island is a geological oddity very similar to Atiu. Like Atiu the central hills are surrounded by an outer rim of raised coral reef known as the *makatea*. The lagoon inside the fringing coral reef is very narrow and shallow.

Only scrub and coconut palms grow on the makatea although Oneroa, Tamarua and Ivirua, the three main villages, are all right on the coast. Taro swamps are found around the inner edge of the makatea where water collects between the hills and the coral flatlands. The central hills are the most fertile part of the island and they're planted with pineapples. Although the geography is basically similar to Atiu's it is much more dramatic. The makatea rises rapidly from the coast and in most places it drops as a sheer wall to the inner region. There are places where you can climb to the top of the cliff for impressive, uninterrupted views.

Since all the streams and rivers running down from the central hills run into a dead end at the inner cliff of the makatea the Mangaia villages all have water problems. You'll see water tanks beside

many houses, storing the rainwater from the roofs. A World Health Organisation dam and water reservoir was built in 1986. The inner cliff of the makatea is such a major barrier that some of the routes through it are quite spectacular, one of the ones through to Ivirua in particular.

History

Captain Cook claimed the European discovery of Mangaia during his second Pacific voyage. He turned up on 29 March 1777 but since the reception was not the friendliest and it was not possible to find a place to land boats the *Resolution* and *Discovery* sailed on to a more friendly greeting at Atiu.

The reception was even less inviting when John Williams turned up in 1823. The pioneering missionary had left Aitutaki to search for Rarotonga, which he eventually found by way of Atiu. Coming first upon Mangaia he attempted to set Polynesian 'teachers' ashore but the Mangaians were so unfriendly that he quickly dropped the idea and sailed off again. In 1824, however, two Polynesian missionaries were landed on the island and, as elsewhere, the conversion to Christianity was soon underway.

The Mangaians have a strange legend of their early history. Most Polynesian islands have some sort of misty legend

Mangaia Cross Section

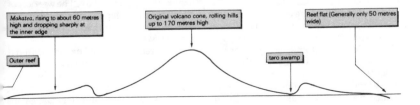

Makatea, rising to about 60 metres high and dropping sharply at the inner edge

Outer reef

Original volcano cone, rolling hills up to 170 metres high

taro swamp

Reef flat (Generally only 50 metres wide)

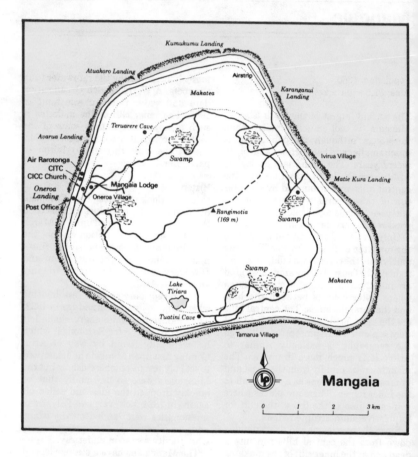

Mangaia

0   1   2   3 km

about a great ancestor arriving on a fantastic canoe. Not the Mangaians: nobody sailed from anywhere to settle Mangaia. Rongo, the father of Mangaia, simply rose from the deep complete with his three sons, to found the island.

The island's name is comparatively recent – it's thought to have been bestowed upon the island only a few years before Cook's visit and means 'peace' or 'temporal power'. The name apparently relates to the interminable battles between the island's various groups and the peace which was finally established when one

leader eventually achieved *mangaia* or power over the whole island.

The Mangaians have a reputation for being a dour, unfriendly lot, an attribute which perhaps helped to keep the aggressive Atiuans at bay. The warriors of Atiu wreaked havoc on Mauke and Mitiaro but never had much success against Mangaia.

More recently Mangaia has suffered from a dramatic population decline. Since the mid-70s the population of the island, stable for some time at around 2000, has fallen by a third. The Mangaians have positively and consistently refused to have anything to do with the central Land Court's attempts to administer land disputes.

Information
Mangaia is a long way from Rarotonga – electricity only arrived in late '85. Although Mangaian ceremonial adzes are a well-known Pacific artefact in world museums the only commonly available handiworks are the *pupu ei's* which you are likely to be garlanded with on departure. The tiny shells with which the *eis* are made can only be found after rainfall. They're black and are found on the makatea, not by the the water. Boiling them in caustic soda produces the typical yellow colour although they can also be grilled to make them white, or dyed a variety of colours. They're then individually pierced with a needle and threaded to make the finished *ei*. It's a time consuming business. In Rarotonga *pupu eis* from Mangaia fetch as much as NZ$25 a dozen.

Despite their reputation and although some Mangaians may initially seem somewhat reserved you'll probably find them quite friendly!

Rangimotia & Island Walk
Rangimotia (169 metres) is the highest point in the island. It's not a straight-forward peak, more of a high plateau. You know you're at the top but you have to explore in several directions to see all the coast. From the Oneroa side of the island there's a track – suitable for motorcycles, four-wheel drives, even regular cars with a little difficulty – right to the top. At the top the track forks and you can follow either fork down to Ivirua village on the east coast.

The tracks follow the ridges of Mangaia's rolling hills and even when they're indistinct it's easy to find your way. Further down the houses in Ivirua come into view and if you take the right track you reach Ivirua through a spectacular cut through the makatea.

From Ivirua you can turn south and

Natives of Mangaia

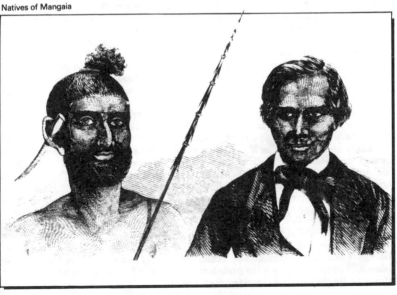

Mangaian Hut

walk to Tamarua, the third village on the island. The trail runs just inland from the makatea for most of the distance. Along this stretch the makatea is not edged with much of a cliff but shortly after the trail climbs back onto the raised coral there is an impressive drop and at a point shortly before Tamarua you can turn off the road for a view over an area of taro swamp. From Tamarua the road runs close to the coast with numerous paths down to the reef. Or you can take the shorter direct route back to Oneroa.

This a pleasant but quite long day's walk. It's probably more than 25 km in total. There's no chance of going thirsty or hungry along the way as long as you have your Swiss Army Knife handy – coconuts, papaya, passionfruit, bananas and, of course, pineapples, can be found along the way.

Caves

The makatea is riddled with caves but the largest and most spectacular is Teruarere. George Tuara who works at the Cook Islands Trading Company is the guide for this cave. He charges NZ$10 and you may

have to ask his boss to let him off work to go with you! The caves were used for burial in the distant past but were rediscovered in the 1930s by George's grandfather and Robert Dean Frisbie – see the introductory Books section. Teruarere means 'jump' (because people used to jump down into the cave opening?).

You do have to climb down into the opening. There's a tree whose branches emerge at ground level and at the other end of this opening chasm there's a fine and frightening view out from the makatea cliff. As you enter, the high, narrow cliffs seem to close overhead. At first there are several small openings high above you and a tree root winds down through one to floor level. Then you have to slither through a low, muddy opening and the cave becomes much more enclosed.

This is a very dramatic cave and most of the time it is very high although fairly narrow. There are glistening-white stalactites and stalagmites but the most interesting feature is simply how far it continues. There are no major side chambers but the main cavern simply continues on and on. It fact it goes so far you have to start out fairly early in the day if you want to explore a reasonable amount. George reckons that it continues at least two km. Although he has been going into the cave for nearly 50 years he has never reached the end.

There are numerous other caves all over the island and several legendary ones no one has yet discovered. One is said to contain the bones of ancient Mangaians of gigantic size. Another, the legendary cave of Piriteumeume, is said to be filled with the skeletons of countless Mangaian warriors, each with his weapons laid beside him.

Other

There are typical, old CICC churches in Oneroa, Ivirua and Tamarua. Look for the sennet rope binding on the roof beams in the Tamarua and Oneroa churches. In front of the Oneroa church is an interesting monument detailing the ministers, both *papa'a* and Maori, of the church and also the Mangaian ministers who have worked as missionaries abroad.

Mangaia has numerous pre-missionary *maraes* but you'd need a local expert to find them. There are countless little beaches and bays around the coastline although nowhere is there good swimming. The reef is very shallow and generally close to the coast. Lake Tiriara is the one lake on the island but it's difficult to distinguish it from the surrounding swamp. There are several landings around the coastline but Avarua, just north of Oneroa towards the airport, is the main shipping harbour.

Places to Stay & Eat

Oneroa consists of one road along the coast, a road up from the coast through a cutting in the makatea and a couple of roads along the coastal edge of the makatea. The government run *Mangaia Lodge* is on the edge of the makatea but after a visitor complained about the standards in mid-86 tourists have no longer been allowed to stay! If you could get in it would cost NZ$40 a night including one meal – there are no cooking facilities – so it's not good value.

There are several families who take

Mangaia

paying guests, typically charging NZ$25 a night including meals. Air Rarotonga will arrange this accommodation for you: you can try Mrs Kareroa or Mr Kaokao Raeora, both on the road up from the makatea cutting.

If you're staying long you might want to bring some of your own food with you. There's a Cook Islands Trading Company store down on the coast road and several other trade stores around. There's a bakery by the school and the steps up from the coast road to the top of the makatea.

Getting There

Air Rarotonga fly to Mangaia for NZ$85 one-way. The 203 km flight takes 40 minutes. You can also use the Silk & Boyd shipping services.

Getting Around

There's no regular motorcycle hire on Mangaia although you could probably arrange something as there are plenty of motorcycles about. Walking is fine, especially the route across the island via Rangimotia, but the distances around the coast are quite long and you can't count on getting a ride from a passing vehicle as there is so little traffic. I walked all the way from Ivirua via Tamarua to Oneroa, several hours' walk, and only saw one truck passing by – the wrong way.

Mauke, Mitiaro & Palmerston

Mauke

Population: 675
Area: 18.4 square km

Mauke is the most easterly of the Cook Islands. It's one of the more easily visited islands since there is a fairly regular flight schedule and it can be combined with a visit to Atiu, its physically similar and once dominant sister island just 92 km away. Mauke, Mitiaro and Atiu are sometimes referred to by the collective name Nga Pu Toru, 'The Three Roots'.

Geology
Like Atiu, Mangaia and Mitiaro this island is a raised atoll with a surrounding *makatea*. Inland from this fossil coral reef there is a band of swampland surrounding the fertile central land. Mauke is like Mitiaro as the central area of the island is flat, rising virtually no higher than the makatea. In contrast to Atiu and Mangaia where the central area is hilly, Mauke rises barely 30 metres above sea level at its highest point. Like Atiu and Mangaia there are numerous limestone caves in the makatea.

History
Mauke takes its name from its legendary founder Uke: the name means 'land of Uke'. Prior to the arrival of Christianity Mauke was totally dominated by the island of Atiu. The Atiuans would descend on murderous, cannibal raids.

Akaina, an Atiuan chieftain, settled on Mauke and spirited away the wife of an island chief. Swearing revenge the jilted chief killed Akaina and most of his compatriots but one escaped and in a small canoe made the perilous crossing to Atiu. Incensed by this affront to Atiuan

power Rongomatane, the great chief of Atiu, set out for Mauke at the head of a fleet of 80 war canoes. The terrified Maukeans took refuge in caves but many of them were hauled out, beaten to death with clubs, cooked and eaten. Satisfied that justice had been done Rongomatane installed an Atiuan named Tararo as chief and sailed back to Atiu.

The surviving islanders regrouped, however, and under Maiti attacked the Atiuans. Unfortunately for the Maukeans Tararo survived and once again an emissary sailed off to alert Rongomatane. And once again the Atiuan war canoes sallied forth to Mauke. This time the Atiuans showed at least some restraint and spared a number of the women and children, taking them back to Atiu as slaves, the cooked flesh of their husbands and fathers accompanying them in the canoes.

The European discovery of Mauke is credited to the pioneering missionary John Williams who arrived on Mauke on 23 June 1823. And who accompanied Mr Williams? Why none other than that unpleasant previous visitor, Rongomatane! It's hardly surprising that the Maukeans were converted to Christianity with an ease and speed that astonished the western visitors. Despite western influence Mauke remained subject to Atiu with *ariki* appointed from Atiu.

Author and island personality Julian Dashwood (*Rakau*) lived for years on Mauke where he ran the island store. See the introductory Books section for more information. His second book, *Today is Forever*, is largely about Mauke.

Economy & Crafts
Mauke's economic development has been erratic. Growing ginger has been a failure and citrus plantations have also been unsuccessful. A handful of cattle are

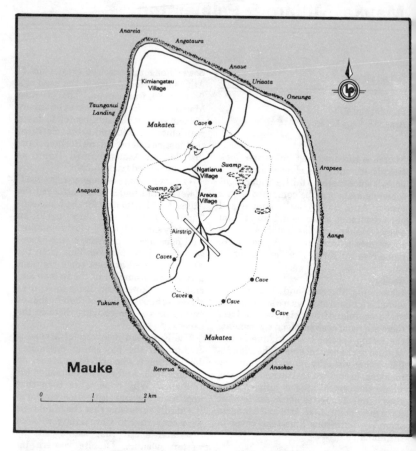

Mauke

Anareia
Angataura
Anaue
Uriaata
Oneunga
Kimiangatau Village
Taunganui Landing
Makatea
Cave
Arapaea
Swamp
Ngatiarua Village
Swamp
Areora Village
Anaputa
Airstrip
Aanga
Caves
Cave
Tukume
Caves
Cave
Cave
Makatea
Rererua
Anaokae

0   1   2 km

raised. Mauke is noted for its pandanus mats and hats and the *kete* baskets. Bowls shaped like the leaves of the breadfruit tree and carved from *miro* wood are another traditional Maukean craft.

The People of Mauke

On one of their murderous forays to Mauke the Atiuans tempted the unfortunate inhabitants out of their cave hideaways by claiming they were on a friendly visit and inviting them (the Maukeans) to a feast that they (the Atiuans) were setting up. This was not totally untrue, as

the foolish people of Mauke found, but they did not anticipate their role at the feast. They were henceforth labelled *Mauke kaa-kaa* or 'Mauke the easily fooled'.

Some say that when deciding which women to eat, the Atiuans always ate the ugliest and spared the most beautiful, which accounts for the extraordinary beauty of Maukean women today!

The Divided Church

Mauke has two villages in the centre, Areora and Ngatiarua, and one on the coast, Kimiangatau. The coastal village was built in 1904 because some of the Maukeans had decided to become Roman Catholics and could no longer tolerate living with those who still followed the London Missionary Society.

Religious disputes were nothing new to the Maukeans as the 1882 CICC church illustrates. At that time there were still just two villages and they got together to build the church. When the outside was complete, however, the two sides could not agree on how the inside should be fitted out. Eventually the argument became so acrimonious that the only solution was to build a wall down the middle and let each village have it's own church within the church.

A new pastor eventually managed to convince his congregations that this was hardly the spirit of neighbourly Christianity and the wall was removed, but the two sides of the church are still decorated in different styles and each village has its own entrance. Inside, the two villages each sit on their own side of the aisle and they take turns singing the hymns! The pulpit, with old Chilean dollars set into the railing, is centrally placed but there's a dividing line down the middle and the minister is expected to straddle the line at all times. The interior of the church is painted in soft, pastel colours.

Beaches

A road runs right around the coast of Mauke, a total distance of 18 km. The fringing reef platform is narrow but Teoneroa beach is fairly good as is the beach at Arapaea Landing on the east side of the island. The beaches on the south side of the island like Anaokae are pleasantly secluded.

Caves

Like Atiu and Mangaia the makatea is riddled with limestone caves. Motuanga Cave or the 'Cave of a Hundred Rooms' is the best known cave on the island. Other important caves are Vai Ou, Vai Tunamea and Vai Moraro or Vaitaongo Cave which is only a 10-minute walk from Ngatiarua. Moti Cave is near the airstrip. Several of the caves are filled with water and it is possible to swim in them.

Places to Stay & Eat

The *Tiare Holiday Cottage* has two sleeping cottages and a separate cooking and shower block. Costs are NZ$16 for a single, NZ$25 for a double, NZ$36 for a triple and NZ$46 for a quadruple. Cook Islandair will book for you. The electricity on Mauke goes off at 10.30 pm.

Getting There

Cook Islandair fly between Rarotonga and Mauke, usually continuing to Atiu before returning to Raro. Unlike the airstrips on Atiu and Mangaia, Mauke's airstrip is up in the central 'highlands' rather than down on the narrow coastal strip. Silk & Boyd ships also operate to Mauke.

Te Rongo and his Three Sons

Mitiaro

Population: 256
Area: 22.3 square km

Mitiaro is another of the southern islands with a raised outer plain or makatea. Like Mauke, but to an even greater degree, the interior of the island is very flat. In fact much of the interior of Mitiaro is a swamp. Two parts of this swamp are deep enough to be labelled as lakes: Rotonui which is the larger, and Rotoiti. Mitiaro's eels are a renowned delicacy. Despite all this swamp the island suffers from severe shortages of fresh water, furthermore the south and east of the island are rocky and desolate. All in all Mitiaro is not a particularly attractive place despite its pleasant lagoon and long stretches of beach.

History
Like Mauke the island of Mitiaro was subject to repeated raids from Atiu, but unlike the Maukeans the Mitiaroans did not hide in caves. They stoutly defended their fortress Te Pari but were, nevertheless, eventually overcome by the Atiuans.

The Reverend John Williams arrived on Mitiaro on 29 July 1823 accompanied by Rongomatane as he had been on Mauke. The small and declining population that lives on Mitiaro today is thought to be entirely descended from raiding Atiuan warriors. Atiuan raids continued, even after the arrival of Christianity, into the 1840s.

The CICC Church
The inhabitants of Mitiaro are now concentrated in one settlement on the west coast. The white-painted CICC church with its blue trim, parquet ceiling decorated with black and white stars, and stained glass windows is a fine sight and the singing on Sundays is superb.

Beaches, Marae & Fort
Mitiaro has some wonderful stretches of beach and the reef at low tide is excellent all around the island. Mitiaro has some ancient remains including *marae* platforms in the south of the island, just north-east of Teunu. They're marked by upright slabs of coral. Also just off the trail to Teunu are the indistinct remains of the ancient Te Pare fort, built as a defence against Atiuan raids. You'd need a local guide to find the traces.

Caves
In common with the other islands with makatea there are a number of caves. Vai Tamaroa and Vai Naure are off the road leading to the airstrip. Vai Ai or the Sandalwood Cave is in the north of the island and has a good freshwater swimming hole. It's reached by a winding track. You can also swim in Vai Marere which is only a 10-minute walk from the village on the Takaue road.

Lakes
It's hard to tell where the surrounding swamps end and the lakes begin. They're hard to approach and although the water is clear the lake bottoms are horribly muddy. As you get closer to the lakes the ground becomes increasingly soggy and wallows unsteadily under your feet. It's probably easier to approach Lake Rotonui than Lake Rotoiti as there's a walking

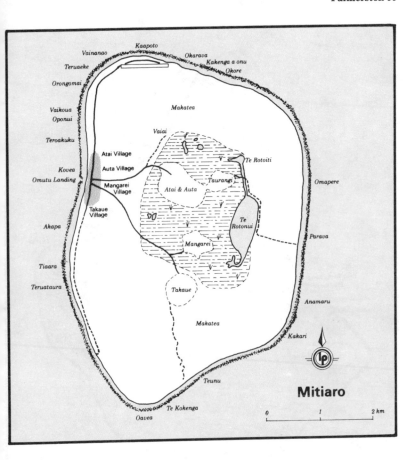

Mitiaro

trail inland from Parava to Lake Rotonui. Small edible fish proliferate in the lake as do the island's famous eels.

Places to Stay & Eat

With its very small population, facilities are extremely limited on Mitiaro. Limited supplies are available at the island stores but it's wise to bring some with you, particularly bread. Mitiaro's dried bananas wrapped in banana leaves (*pieres*) are a delicacy in Rarotonga. The only electricity on Mitiaro is from individual generators.

Getting There

Cook Islandair fly to Mitiaro but only about once a week.

Palmerston

Population: 51
Area: 2.0 square km

Palmerston is something of a Cook Islands oddity: it's only a little north of Aitutaki, otherwise the most northerly of

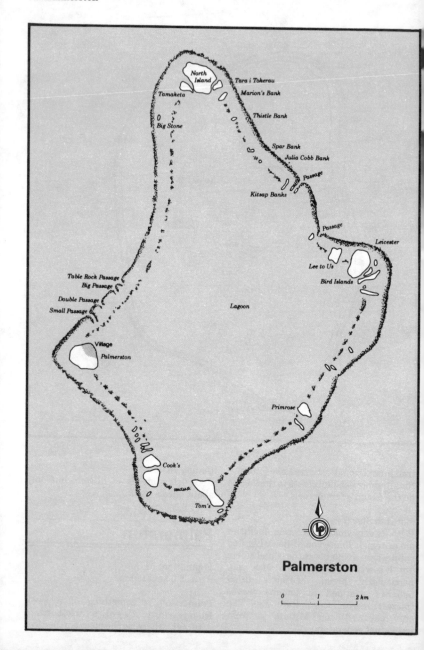

North Island

Tara i Toherau

Tamaketa

Marion's Bank

Thistle Bank

Big Stone

Spar Bank

Julia Cobb Bank

Passage

Kitsap Banks

Passage

Leicester

Lee to Us

Table Rock Passage

Bird Islands

Big Passage

Double Passage

Small Passage

Lagoon

Village

Palmerston

Primrose

Cook's

Tom's

Palmerston

0   1   2 km

the southern group, but it's also far to the west of the other southern islands. Furthermore it's an atoll like the northern group islands and unlike the other southern islands. As a result it sometimes gets treated as part of the northern group.

The lagoon is 11 km wide at its widest point and 35 small islands dot the reef. At low tide the lagoon is completely closed off. Visiting ships have to anchor outside the reef.

History

Captain Cook sighted the island in 1774 when it was unpopulated. He did not stop on that occasion but in 1777 when he passed by on his third voyage his ships did pause and boats were sent ashore to seek provisions.

A passing missionary ship en route to Tahiti stopped at Palmerston in 1797 and in 1811 another ship stopped to collect beche de mer and shark fins, which are valued as delicacies by Chinese. The Tahitians talked of using the island as a place of banishment for criminals but it remained uninhabited.

In 1850 the crew of the *Merchant of Tahiti* discovered four starving Europeans on the island. When he took them to Rarotonga the ship's captain laid claim to the island, then passed the claim to a Scottish trader in Tahiti named John Branden. This gentlemen placed a representative on the island and some time later discovered William Marsters, a European, living on Manuae island and persuaded him to move to Palmerston in 1863.

William Marsters became a living legend. The present inhabitants of the island are all Marsters descended from William and his three Polynesian wives. They not only populated Palmerston: to this day you'll find people with the surname Marsters all over the Cooks and it's a common name on cemetery headstones. Old William Marsters died in 1899 and is buried near his original homestead.

At one time the population of the island was as high as 150 but it's a quiet and little visited place today.

The Northern Group

The northern islands of the Cooks are scattered coral atolls, specks of land in a vast expanse of sea. They are all low-lying and from a ship cannot even be seen from much more than 10 km away. On many of the islands severe hurricanes will send waves right across the islands. Although atolls such as these are the romantic image of a Pacific island – complete with sandy beaches, clear and shallow lagoons, swaying palm trees – in actual fact life is hard on an atoll. Fish may be abundant in the lagoon but atoll soil is only marginally fertile and the range of foodstuffs which can be grown is very limited. Fresh water is always a problem. Shallow wells are often the only source of drinking water and the supply is generally limited and often not very pleasant to drink.

In the modern world atoll life has another drawback apart from these natural ones and that is sheer isolation. Today people want economic opportunity, education for their children and contact with the outside world. On a tiny island where the only physical contact is a trading ship coming through a couple of times a year these things are clearly not available and at the same time returning islanders and the radio whet the appetite for the outside world. Many of the northern islands are suffering from a declining population.

If you want to visit islands of the northern group the only regular way of getting there is on the Silk & Boyd ships – see the introductory Getting Around chapter for fare details. The ships generally unload and load at the islands by day so if you're doing a circuit of the islands you can spend a day or more on a number of islands. If you want to stay longer you're generally stuck with waiting until the next ship comes by – which may be months away.

Although there is no regular accommodation on any of the northern islands the infrequent visitors are usually made

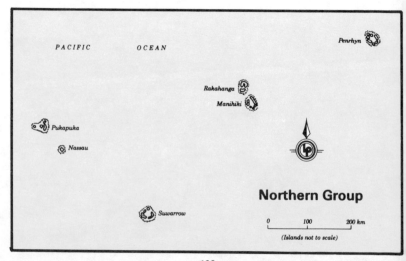

PACIFIC   OCEAN

Penrhyn

Rakahanga
Manihiki

Pukapuka

Nassau

Suwarrow

Northern Group

0   100   200 km

(Islands not to scale)

welcome and some arrangement will always be made. Plan to pay your way, however, both in cash terms and with food or other supplies. Food supplies are always limited on the islands and the arrival of a ship is always a major occasion.

For an account of a short visit to various northern islands via the Silk & Boyd ships look for *Lost & Found in the Cook Islands* (Pukapuka, Nassau and Palmerston) or *Across the South Pacific* (Manihiki and Rakahanga).

Manihiki

Population: 396
Area: 5.4 square km

This is reputed to be one of the most beautiful atolls in the Pacific. Nearly 40 islands, some of them little more than tiny *motus*, encircle the four km wide and totally enclosed lagoon. The main village is Tauhunu but there is a second village, Tukao.

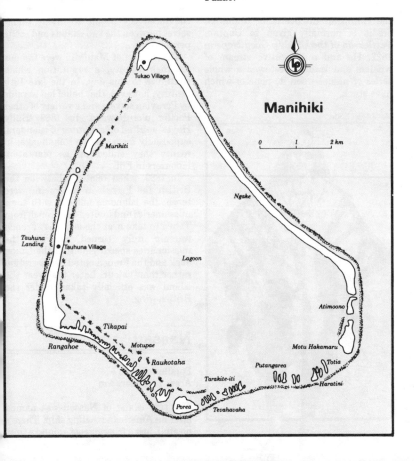

Manihiki has no safe anchorage for visiting ships which consequently stay offshore. What it does have is pearl shells which are the mainstay of the island and a significant export for the Cook Islands. The abilities of the island's pearl divers are legendary – they can dive effortlessly to great depths and stay submerged for minutes at a time. Manihiki was formerly owned by the people of Rakahanga – see the Rakahanga section for more details.

History

Although some authorities consider that the Spanish explorer Pedro Quiros was the European discoverer of Manihiki, credit is normally given to Captain Patrickson of the US ship *Good Hope* in 1822. He and a successive stream of whalers and traders bestowed a whole series of names upon it, none of which have stuck.

Manihikian Bride

The missions came to Manihiki in 1849 after a Manihiki canoe en route to Rakahanga was blown off course, rescued by a whaler and left at Manuae. The missionaries took the canoe passengers back to Manihiki and left two Polynesian teachers at the same time. They also left disease. The ensuing epidemic quickly convinced the islanders that they had not been behaving themselves and should embrace Christianity.

Manihiki at that time was more-or-less a subsidiary of Rakahanga and the people of Rakahanga 'commuted' to Manihiki as necessary. In 1852 the missionaries convinced the people to divide themselves between the two islands and settle permanently.

The women of Manihiki were famous for their beauty, a reputation which continues to this day. In the late 19th century, however, that belief led to raids by Peruvian slavers and a variety of other Pacific n'er-do-wells. In 1869 'Bully Hayes' spirited off a number of islanders, supposedly for a visit to Rakahanga; in reality they ended up as plantation labourers in Fiji.

In 1889, when relations between the British and French in the Pacific were tense, the islanders fell out with their missionaries and invited the French from Tahiti to take over the island. A French warship duly turned up but the missionaries speedily hoisted the Union Jack and the French opted for discretion rather than valour. Later that year the island was officially taken under the British wing.

Nassau

Population: 133
Area: 1.2 square km

The tiny island of Nassau was named after an American whaling ship. There's no atoll, just a fringing reef around a tiny, half km long, sand cay. There is a coconut plantation and taro is grown in the centre of the island.

History

Only 88 km south-east of Pukapuka the island was effectively the property of the Pukapukans. It was probably first discovered by Europeans in 1803 and each successive visitor gave it a new name, usually that of the discovering ship. For some reason, however, it was the American whaler *Nassau's* visit, comparatively late in the day in 1835, which gave the island its present name.

The island did not have a permanent population although occasional groups from other islands stopped for longer or shorter periods. An American attempted to grow coconuts and other plants from 1876 and in later years a number of European-owned copra plantations were established. In 1945 these were sold to the colonial government for £2000. Six years later they were sold to the chiefs of Pukapuka for the same figure; their temporary work groups have become a virtually permanent population.

Penrhyn

Population: 607
Area: 9.8 square km

Penrhyn is the most northerly of the Cook Islands and its lagoon is unlike most of the other Cook atolls in that it is very wide and easily accessible. From Omoka, one main village, Te Tautua, the other main village, isn't visible accept for its church roof. Not only is the lagoon accessible to ships, it also has plenty of sharks although most are harmless. For an interesting account of the island's history during the last century see *Impressions of Tongareva* – 1816-1901 from the University of the South Pacific (Suva, Fiji, 1984).

Penrhyn was famous throughout the Pacific at one time for its natural mother of pearl which is still found to this day. Some interesting shell jewellery is also produced and Penrhyn is noted for its fine *rito* hats.

History

Polynesian legends relate that the island was fished up from the depths of the ocean by Vatea, the eldest son of the great mother in Avaiki. He used a fish-hook baited with a star but when that did not work he tore a piece of flesh from his thigh, baited the hook with that and promptly pulled up the island from the deep. He then hung the hook in the sky. Although the local name Tongareva is still widely used the atoll takes its most un-Polynesian name from the British ship *Lady Penrhyn* which dropped by in 1788 on the way back to England from Australia. The ship was one of the 11 which carried the original convict settlers out to Sydney in Australia. The Maori name Tongareva could translate as something like 'to the south of the great emptiness' – there's a lot of nothing to the north of Penrhyn – or 'Tonga floating in space'. Another Maori name, Mangarongaro, is also sometimes used although some people say it was originally only the name of one of the islands in the atoll. There is no direct translation but a *mangaro* is a kind of coconut.

After the *Lady Penrhyn* it was 28 years before a visit by the Russian ship *Rurick* in 1816. The earliest western accounts of Penrhyn all comment on the unusual fierceness and erratic behaviour of the inhabitants of Penrhyn. The following extract is a typical description from a visit by the US ship *Porpoise* in 1841:

... each and all of them were talking in a language altogether unintelligible and in voices peculiarly harsh and discordant accompanying their words with every unimaginable contortion of the body and with the most diabolical expressions of countenance

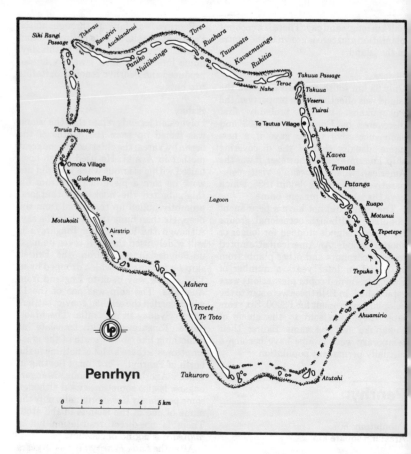

Penrhyn

0 1 2 3 4 5 km

every muscle being brought into play and made to quiver apparently with rage & excitement, and their eyes fairly starting from their heads. It is utterly impossible for the mind to conceive and altogether out of my power to find words to express or convey any adequate idea of a scene so savage ....

None of these early visitors dared to go ashore and they all tried to keep the inhabitants distinctly at arms length. Despite this impression when the American ship *Chatham* ran onto the reef in 1853 to the surprise and relief of the crew and passengers they were treated well. Some of them were to remain on the island for almost a year before being rescued. E H Lamont, the trader who had chartered the unfortunate vessel, wrote *Wild Life among the Pacific Islanders* about his time on the island. He obviously entered into atoll life wholeheartedly because he married three women while he was there! Dr R in his account was the Dr Longghost of Herman Melville's *Omoo*.

The first missionaries arrived in 1854 and those warlike and terrifying islanders quickly became obedient churchgoers. So obedient that the four Polynesian teachers landed by the missionaries 'sold' their flock to Peruvian slavers in 1862-63. They netted $5 a head and went along to South America as overseers for a salary of $100 a month. The island's population was decimated by the activities of the slavers who dubbed the island 'the island of the four evangelists'. That disastrous slaving foray left Penrhyn with a population of only 88. It had rebounded to 445 by 1902 but the entire chiefly line disappeared during this period so today Penrhyn is the only island in the Cooks with no *ariki* or paramount chief.

Like Rakahanga, Penrhyn has an unused airstrip as a result of its use as an American, WW II airbase. The airstrip is on the island of Omoka but it's too far from the southern islands to be flown to regularly. The remains of the *Go-Gettin' Gal*, a four-engined bomber, still remain there although it's gradually being used up as a source of scrap metal.

Pukapuka

Population: 788
Area: 5.1 square km

Shaped like a three-bladed fan Pukapuka's atoll has an island at each 'blade end' and another in the middle. The northernmost island gives its name to the whole atoll although it is also known, usually in parentheses, as 'Wale'. The only landing place is reached by narrow and difficult passages through the reef on the western side of Wale Island.

There are three villages – Ngake, Roto and Yato – all on Wale Island. Copra and smaller quantities of bananas and papayas are grown. The relative proximity to Samoa has resulted in the islanders' customs and language relating more closely to Samoa than to the rest of the Cooks. There is a notably decorated Catholic church on the island and excellent swimming and snorkelling, particularly off the central island of Kotawa. Pukapuka is noted for its finely woven mats.

History

Early legends relate tales of the island rising from the deep with men inside it or of great voyages. Another tale tells of a great tidal wave about 400 years ago which left only two women and 15 men alive on the island; with considerable effort (on the women's part!) they managed to repopulate it. There may have been some truth in this tale as the islanders recall that it was during the rule of the fourth chief after the great disaster that the first western visitors arrived.

That first western visitor was the Spanish explorer Alvaro de Mendana who, with his navigator Pedro Fernandez de Quiros, sailed from Peru in 1595 and later that year discovered an island which

Soul Traps in Pukapuka

he named San Bernardo. Although they did not attempt to land nor did they see signs of life it is generally accepted that the island they sighted was Pukapuka. Over 150 years later in 1765 the British ships *Dolphin* and *Tamar* again sighted the islands and again decided against attempting a landing due to the high surf. They named the atoll the Islands of Danger and Pukapuka is still sometimes referred to as Danger Island.

Further sightings and namings continued and finally in 1857 Polynesian missionaries were landed, followed in 1862 by a visit by the pioneer missionary William Wyatt Gill. A year later the population of the island was decimated by slave raids from Peru. In 1865 the London Missionary Society ship *John Williams* which had spent so much time in this region was wrecked on Pukapuka's reef.

During this century South Seas character Robert Dean Frisbie lived for some time on the island and wrote *The Book of Pukapuka*, published in 1929. His daughter Johnny Frisbie also wrote of the island in *Miss Ulysses from Pukapuka*, published in 1948. Modern maps of Pukapuka are still based on Robert Dean Frisbie's 1925 survey.

Rakahanga

Population: 271
Area: 4.1 square km

Only 42 km north of Manihiki this rectangular atoll is almost completely enclosed by two major islands and a host of smaller *motus*. Without the pearl wealth of Manihiki the island is conspicuously quieter and less energetic. Copra is the only export product although the islanders grow breadfruit and a taro-

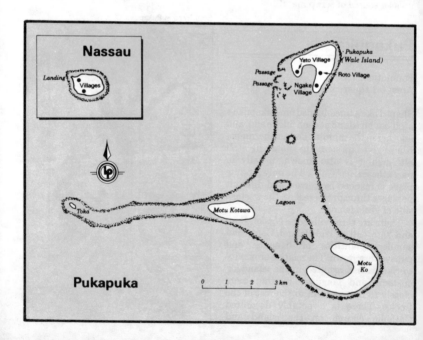

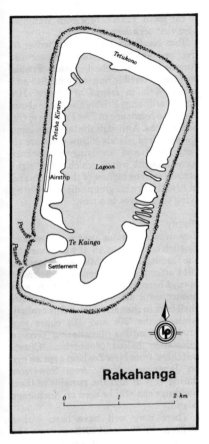

Rakahanga

0   1   2 km

and the island of Manihiki breaking off from the island and drifting away. There are a variety of similar legends including one which tells of the island subsequently being populated entirely by the offspring of one man and his wife, the man taking his four daughters as additional wives.

In 1606 the commander of the ships *Capitana* and *Almiranta*, Pedro Fernandez de Quiros, who as navigator to Mendana had already discovered Pukapuka 10 years earlier, sighted the island. He reported that the islanders were:

the most beautiful white and elegant people that were met during the voyage.

Furthermore, he continued, the women were exceptionally beautiful and:

if properly dressed, would have advantages over our Spanish women.

Such reports were no doubt the genesis for many romantic notions of the South Seas! De Quiros was not the only member of the expedition to be impressed. A Franciscan friar accompanying the expedition named the discovery the island of Gente Hermosa, 'beautiful people'. At this time Rakahanga and Manihiki were both owned by the people of Rakahanga who used to 'commute' between the two islands.

Over 200 years were to pass before the island was again visited by western ships, first a Russian expedition in 1820 then a series of whalers and trading ships. As usual a number of easily forgotten names were bestowed on the island. In 1849 Polynesian missionaries arrived on Manihiki, although at that time it was still only settled by temporary groups from Rakahanga. The often hazardous journey between the two islands resulted in numerous deaths at sea and in 1852 the missionaries convinced the islanders to divide themselves between the two atolls. Travelling between Manihiki and Rakahanga can still be dangerous.

like vegetable. The *rito* hats woven on Manihiki are particularly fine. The population is concentrated in the village of Nivano on the south-west corner of the atoll.

Rakahanga has an airstrip but in common with Penrhyn, the other northern island with this luxury, the cost of flying from Rarotonga is so excessive that it is rarely used.

History

Legends tell of Rakahanga being hauled up from under the sea by three brothers

Lost En Route

Although missionaries tried as early as 1852 to put an end to voyaging back and forth across the 40-odd km between Rakahanga and Manihiki, people continue to shuttle back and forth, sometimes with harrowing results. In June 1953, for example, nine islanders set out at night to sail from Manihiki to Rakahanga. Come the dawn they were lost: a squall had blown them off course and where they were relative to the two islands was a mystery. Where they were relative to Pukapuka, 500 km downwind, didn't seem to be such a mystery because they set out to sail there. Five days later, in an extraordinary navigational feat, they arrived in Pukapuka.

In 1965 another small boat from Manihiki suffered engine failure midway between the islands and was swept away to the west by the steady three to four knot current that runs between the islands. Sixty-five days and almost 3500 km later the crew landed at Erromanga in Vanuatu. The book *The Man who Refused to Die* recounts the tale of this extraordinary voyage and the persistence of Techu Makimare, the hero of the crew.

Suwarrow

Population: 0
Area: 0.4 square km

The unpopulated atoll of Suwarrow is one of the best known in the whole Cook Islands group due to a prolonged visit by one man. Between 1952 and his death in 1977 New Zealander Tom Neale lived on the island for extended periods as a virtual hermit and his book, *An Island to Oneself* became a South Seas classic. If you want to know all about how to live on an atoll then this book is a must.

Although Tom Neale is long gone – he was buried in the cemetery opposite Rarotonga's airport – his memory lives on and yachties often call in to the atoll. It's one of the few in the northern Cooks with an accessible lagoon. Tom's room is still furnished just as it was when he lived there. Visiting yachts fill in a logbook left

in the room. Pearl divers from Manihiki also visit occasionally.

Tom Neale wasn't the only writer to live on, and write about, Suwarrow. American-born Robert Dean Frisbie survived a terrible hurricane in 1942 and wrote of it in *Island of Desire*. His daughter Johnny Frisbie also wrote about the same hurricane in *The Frisbies of the South Seas*. Although the lagoon is large the scattered islands of Suwarrow are all very small and low-lying. Hurricanes have brought waves which wash right across even the highest of the islands and in 1942 the Frisbie group only survived by tying themselves to a tree.

History

Suwarrow's curious name is neither English nor Polynesian. It was named by the Russian explorer Mikhail Lazarev in 1814 after his ship *Suvarov*. Nor has it always been uninhabited. There was an unsuccessful attempt to produce pearl shell here in the early part of this century while in the '20s and '30s copra was produced until a devastating termite infestation halted production. 'Coast-watchers' from New Zealand kept an eye on Japanese activity from Suwarrow during WW II and the remains of their buildings can still be seen on Anchorage Island.

There may well have been earlier visitors. In the mid-19th century the American whaler *Gem* was wrecked on the reef. A ship came from Tahiti to salvage the whaler's oil cargo and one of the visiting ship's officers dug up a box containing $15,000. Where this cache came from has never been satisfactorily explained although the coins were thought to date from the mid-1700s and may have been connected with the first British Pacific expedition under Commodore George Anson in 1742. In 1876 another visitor found Spanish coins dating from the 1600s.

In 1860 the atoll was the scene of a dramatic and tragic dispute. First, a

Turtle Is
One Tree Is
Brushwood Is
Manu Is
Whale Is
Anchorage Is
Gull Is
Little Patches
Greenlands Benefit
The Seven Is
Baby Patch
Motu Tou
Lewin Reef
Man in the Boat
Perfect Reef
Entrance Is
Marriott Reef
New Is

Suwarrow

0   2   4 km

group of eight people, one of them an Englishman, drifted to Suwarrow after an abortive Manihiki-Rakahanga voyage. Later a group of Penrhyn pearl divers with a European boss turned up and later still another European visitor was left on the atoll. Shortly after the arrival of the third European an argument broke out between the pearl divers and their leader and all three Europeans were murdered.

In the mid-1870s more evidence of an early European visit was discovered when signs of habitation, various artefacts and skeletons were unearthed. Were they left by shipwrecked Spaniards? Or were they the remains of the English crew lost on a cutter from the ship *Pandora*, sent to the Pacific in 1791 to search for the mutineers of the *Bounty*?

Glossary

Ara Metua – ancient Polynesian road around the circumference of Rarotonga: many parts of it still remain, inland from the newer coast road

ariki – high chiefs: traditional head of a district or tribe

beer school – communal drinking session where **bush beer** is consumed

bush beer – locally produced, moonshine beer brewed from oranges, bananas, or pawpaws

CICC – Cook Island Christian Church, the protestant church which continues from the original London Missionary Society churches

copra – coconut 'meat' from which coconut oil is produced, an important product throughout the Pacific. The problem with copra is the price is very volatile – it has reached as high as US$450 a ton but currently is much much lower.

ei kaki – flower leis draped around visitors on arrival or departure

ei katu – flower tiaras

eke – octopus

ika – fish

koutu – ancient Polynesian open-air royal court

LMS – London Missionary Society, the original missionary force in the Cook Islands and in many other regions of the Pacific

mataiapo – head of a sub-tribe, a rank down from an *ariki*

makatea – raised coral reef which forms a coastal plain around several islands of the southern group including Mangaia and Atiu

mana – power or influence

Maori – the Polynesian people of the Cook Islands and also of New Zealand, also the language of these people. Literally means 'indigenous' or 'local'

marae – family or tribal temple

maroro – flying fish

mate – die

motu – lagoon islet

pandanus – type of palm leaf used for thatching the roofs of traditional houses and for baskets, bags and *rito* hats

papa'a – westerners, also the English language

pareu – wrap around sarong-type garment

puku – mollusc which produces pearlshell

rito – hats woven of pandanus or bleached, young palm leaves

tamanu – banyan tree

Tangaroa – corpulent but phallic figure variously known as the god of fertility or the god of the sea; appears on the Cook Island one dollar coin

taramea – crown-of-thorns starfish but colloquially used to refer to bar girls or prostitutes

tiki – symbolic human figure

tivaivai – colourful and intricately sewn applique works which are traditionally made as burial shrouds but are also used as bedspreads or simply as wall hangings. They're very rarely seen for sale

tumunu – hollowed out stump of a coconut tree used to brew **bush beer**

umukai – traditional Polynesian food (*kai*) cooked in an underground (*umu*) oven

wale – traditional house on the island of Pukapuka

Index

Lonely Planet Newsletter

We collect an enormous amount of information here at Lonely Planet. Apart from our research there's a steady stream of letters from people out on the road. To make the most of all this info we produce a quarterly Newsletter (approx Feb, May, Aug, and Nov).

The Newsletter is packed with down-to-earth information from the pens of hundreds of travellers who write from first hand experience. Whether you want the latest facts, travel stories, or simply to reminisce, the Newsletter will keep you in touch with what is going on.

Where else could you find out:
• about boat trips on the Yalu River?
• where to stay if you want to live in a typical Thai village?
• how long it takes to get a Nepalese trekking permit?
• that Israeli youth hostel stamps will get you deported from Syria?
• you don't need a visa for Columbia but you do for Venezuela?

One year's subscription is $10.00 (that's US$ in the USA or A$ in Australia), payable by cheque, money order, Amex, Visa, Bankcard or MasterCard.

Order Form
Please send me four issues of the Lonely Planet Newsletter. (Subscription starts with next issue. Price valid until December 1987.)

Name and address (print) ....

....

....

....

Tick one
☐ Cheque enclosed (payable to Lonely Planet Publications)
☐ Money Order enclosed (payable to Lonely Planet Publications)
Charge my ☐ Amex, ☐ Visa, ☐ Bankcard, ☐ MasterCard for the amount of $ ....

Card No ....

Expiry Date ....

Cardholder's Name (print) ....

Signature .... Date ....

Return this form to:
Lonely Planet Publications   *or*   Lonely Planet Publications
PO Box 2001A   PO Box 88
Berkeley   South Yarra
CA 94702   Victoria 3141
USA   Australia

Lonely Planet guides to the Pacific

Australia – a travel survival kit
The complete low-down on Down Under. This is Lonely Planet's home territory so this guide gives you the full story, from the red centre to the coast, from cosmopolitan cities to country towns: how to get around, where to find the best food and accomodation – and koalas.

New Zealand – a travel survival kit
Visitors to New Zealand find a land of fairytale beauty and scenic contrasts – a natural wonderland. This book has information about the places you won't want to miss: glaciers, hot springs, beaches, national parks, and special information on ski-resorts and famous walks.

Tramping in New Zealand
Call it tramping, hiking, walking, bushwalking, or trekking – travelling on your feet is the best way to come to grips with New Zealand's natural beauty. This guide gives detailed descriptions for 20 walks of various length and difficulty.

Fiji – a travel survival kit
This is a comprehensive guide to the Fijian archipelago. On a number of these beautiful islands accommodation ranges from camping grounds to international hotels – whichever you prefer this book will help you to enjoy the South Seas.

Tahiti & French Polynesia – a travel survival kit
The image of palm-fringed beaches and friendly people continues to lure travellers to Polynesia. This book gives you all the facts on paradise, and will be useful whether you plan a package holiday, or to travel the islands independently.

Papua New Guinea – a travel survival kit
Papua New Guinea is truly 'the last unknown' – the last inhabited place on earth to be explored by Europeans. This guide has the latest information for travellers who want to find just how rewarding a trip to this remote and amazing country can be.

Bushwalking in Papua New Guinea
Papua New Guinea offers exciting challenges for bushwalkers. This book describes 11 walks of various length and difficulty, through one of the world's most beautiful, rugged and exotic countries. Specific and practical information is provided.

Lonely Planet guides to South-East Asia

South-East Asia on a shoestring
For over 10 years this has been known as the 'yellow bible' to travellers in South-East Asia. The fifth edition has updated information on Brunei, Burma, Hong Kong, Indonesia, Macau, Malaysia, Papua New Guinea, the Philippines, Singapore, and Thailand.

Indonesia – a travel survival kit
This comprehensive guidebook covers the entire Indonesian archipelago, from Irian Jaya to Sumatra, including Bali and Lombok. Some of the most remarkable sights and sounds in South-East Asia can be found amongst these countless islands and this book has all the facts.

Bali & Lombok – a travel survival kit
Bali is a picturesque tropical island with a fascinating culture and an almost fairytale unreality – dense tropical jungle, superb temples, great beaches and surf, and traditional villages. Lombok is less touched by outside influences and has a special atmosphere of its own.

Malaysia, Singapore and Brunei – a travel survival kit
These three nations offer amazing geographic and cultural variety – from hill stations to beaches, from Dyak longhouses to futuristic cities – this is Asia at its most accessible.

Burma – a travel survival kit
Burma is one of Asia's friendliest and most interesting countries, but for traveller's there's one catch – you can only stay for seven days. This book shows you how to make the most of your visit.

Thailand – a travel survival kit
Beyond the Buddhist temples and Bangkok bars there is much to see in fascinating Thailand. This extensively researched guide presents an inside look at Thailand's culture, people and language.

The Philippines – a travel survival kit
The 7000 islands of the Philippines are a paradise for the adventurous traveller. The friendly Filipinos, colourful festivals, superb natural scenery, and frequent travel connections make island hopping addictive.

Lonely Planet travel guides

Africa on a Shoestring
Alaska – a travel survival kit
Australia – a travel survival kit
Bali & Lombok – a travel survival kit
Bangladesh – a travel survival kit
Burma – a travel survival kit
Bushwalking in Papua New Guinea
Canada – a travel survival kit
China – a travel survival kit
Ecuador & the Galapagos Islands
Fiji – a travel survival kit
Hong Kong, Macau & Canton – a travel survival kit
India – a travel survival kit
Indonesia – a travel survival kit
Japan – a travel survival kit
Kashmir, Ladakh & Zanskar – a travel survival kit
Kathmandu & the Kingdom of Nepal
Korea & Taiwan – a travel survival kit
Malaysia, Singapore & Brunei – a travel survival kit
Mexico – a travel survival kit
New Zealand – a travel survival kit
North-East Asia on a Shoestring
Pakistan – a travel survival kit kit
Papua New Guinea – a travel survival kit
Philippines – a travel survival kit
South America on a Shoestring
South-East Asia on a Shoestring
Sri Lanka – a travel survival kit
Tahiti – a travel survival kit
Thailand – a travel survival kit
Tibet – a travel survival kit
Tramping in New Zealand
Travel with Children
Travellers Tales
Trekking in the Indian Himalaya
Trekking in the Nepal Himalaya
Turkey – a travel survival kit
USA West
West Asia on a Shoestring

Lonely Planet phrasebooks

Indonesia Phrasebook
China Phrasebook
Nepal Phrasebook
Thailand Phrasebook

Lonely Planet travel guides are available around the world. If you can't find them, ask your bookshop to order them from one of the distributors listed below. For countries not listed or if you would like a free copy of our latest booklist write to Lonely Planet in Australia.

Lonely Planet distributors

Australia
Lonely Planet Publications, PO Box 88, South Yarra, Victoria 3141.
Canada
Raincoast Books, 112 East 3rd Avenue, Vancouver, British Columbia V5T 1C8.
Denmark
Scanvik Books aps, Store Kongensgade 59 A, DK-1264 Copenhagen K.
Hong Kong
The Book Society, GPO Box 7804.
India & Nepal
UBS Distributors, 5 Ansari Rd, New Delhi.
Israel
Geographical Tours Ltd, 8 Tverya St, Tel Aviv 63144.
Japan
Intercontinental Marketing Corp, IPO Box 5056, Tokyo 100-31.
Malaysia
MPH Distributors, 13 Jalan 13/6, Petaling Jaya, Selangor.
Netherlands
Nilsson & Lamm bv, Postbus 195, Pampuslaan 212, 1380 AD Weesp.
New Zealand
Roulston Greene Publishing Associates Ltd, Box 33850, Takapuna, Auckland 9.
Pakistan
London Book House, 281/C Tariq Rd, PECHS Karachi 29, Pakistan
Papua New Guinea see Australia
Singapore
MPH Distributors, 3rd Storey, 601 Sims Drive #03-21, Singapore 1438
Spain
Altair, c/o Balmes, 69, Barcelona, 08001.
Sweden
Esselte Kartcentrum AB, Vasagatan 16, S-111 20 Stockholm.
Thailand
Chalermnit, 108 Sukhumvit 53, Bangkok, 10110.
UK
Roger Lascelles, 47 York Rd, Brentford, Middlesex, TW8 0QP.
USA
Lonely Planet Publications, PO Box 2001A, Berkeley, CA 94702.
West Germany
Buchvertrieb Gerda Schettler, Postfach 64, D3415 Hattorf a H.